Meg

Many thanks for
presenting yourself, wedding
consultants and the Association
so favorably on NBC.
We appreciate your support.

Jerry

Meg,
Sharing the spotlight with the likes of
Barbara Faber - how exciting! Thanks for
the plug. You are a real pro.

Eileen

Colors
for Brides

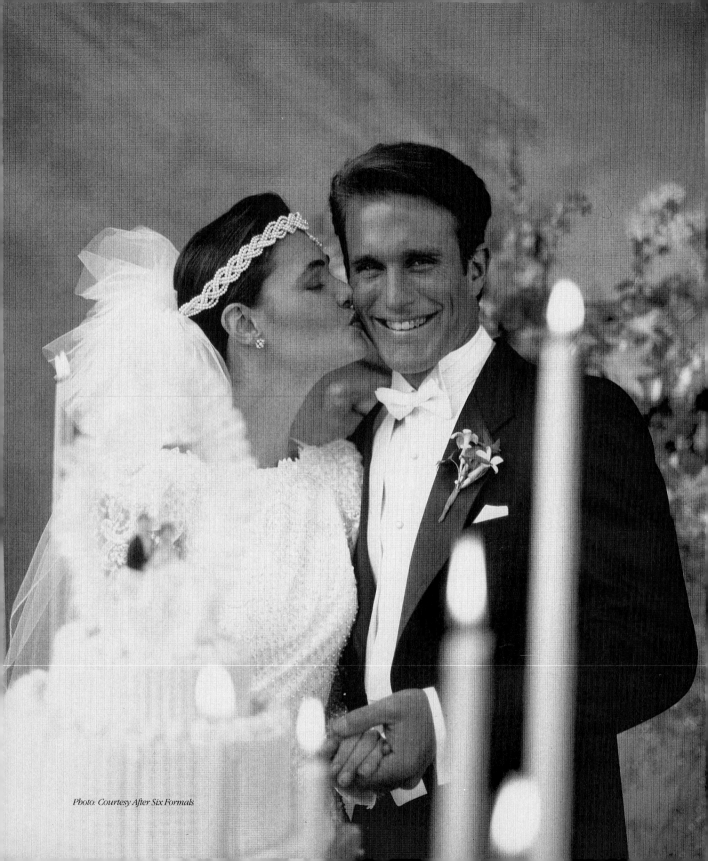

Colors for Brides

Planning Your Wedding,
Your Trousseau and
Your First Home With
Your Seasonal Colors

by Lauren Smith
with Kathleen Hughes

ACROPOLIS BOOKS LTD.
WASHINGTON D.C.

Color Makeup Pages 14-21 by L'Oreal

Production of Photography and Portraits
for L'Oreal, Lydia Munro
Photography
Len Prince
Portrait Artist
Craig Avner
Bridal Apparel
LoVece Ltd.

Models
Click Model Management Inc.
Bethann Management Co.
Hair and Makeup
Joe McDevitt for Kramer & Kramer Inc.
Jewelry
Frank Mastoloni & Sons Inc.

ACROPOLIS BOOKS, LTD.
Kathleen P. Hughes, Publisher
Colortone Building, 2400 17th St., N.W.
Washington, D.C. 20009

Attention: Schools and Corporations
ACROPOLIS books are available at quantity discounts with bulk purchase for educational, business, or sales promotional use. For information, please write to:
SPECIAL SALES DEPARTMENT, ACROPOLIS BOOKS, LTD., 2400 17th St., N.W., WASHINGTON, D.C. 20009.

Are there Acropolis books you want but cannot find in your local stores?
You can get any Acropolis book title in print. Simply send title and retail price. Be sure to add postage and handling: $2.25 for orders up to $15.00, $3.00 for orders from $15.01 to $30.00; $3.75 for orders from $30.01 to $100.00; $4.50 for orders over $100.00. District of Columbia residents add applicable sales tax. Enclose check or money order only, no cash please, to:
ACROPOLIS BOOKS LTD.
2400 17th St., N.W.
WASHINGTON, D.C. 20009

Library of Congress
Cataloging-in-Publication Data
Smith, Lauren.
     Colors for brides: planning your wedding, your trousseau, and your first home with your seasonal colors: includes bridal gift register and color palettes / by Lauren Smith with Kathleen Hughes.
          p.   cm.
     Bibliography: p.
     Includes index.
     ISBN 0-87491-910-X : $24.95
     1. Wedding etiquette. 2. Weddings—United States. 3. Color in weddings. I. Hughes, Kathleen, 1945– . II. Title.
BJ2051.S6   1989
395'.22—dc19   88-30412
                                                                    CIP

Dear Bride-to-be ~

Twenty years ago when I was planning my own wedding, I raced from store to store, all over New York City, searching for my dress, my attendants' dresses, clothes for my trousseau *and* the first furnishings for our first home. I had some knowledge, a lot of intuition, but no plan.

This is when I decided to become a designer. I wanted to understand why some things seemed to go together and others didn't. I wanted to know more about furniture and fashion style. I wanted to delve into design theory . . . and I wanted to know everything *before* my wedding, so it would be the most beautiful ceremony anyone had ever attended.

Of course, it was impossible to learn all this in such a short time. In fact, it has taken me the twenty years since my wedding day to put together the ideas and color theory I give to you, Bride-to-be, in this book.

Now you will have magical color as the key to organizing not only your wedding plans, but your trousseau and home decorating. It is the secret I wish I had known so many years ago. And, I hope it will make your marriage day and your new life as colorful as you wish it to be.

With best wishes for a long and happy life together,

Lauren Smith

With appreciation

To Bob Smith for helping me in everything I do. To all the people at Acropolis: John Hackl, Sandy Trupp, Kathy Cunningham, and especially to Al Hackl and Kathleen Hughes. To Valerie Gardiner (nee Avedon), for holding my hand the second book around. And to all those without whose enthusiasm I would not have written the book—especially Marilyn Bennett, Shelby Buracker, Carole Loetscher, Trish McCurry, Virginia Oakland, Nancy Penn, Linda Petersen-Smith, Marjorie Stratton, Sophia Suda, and Carolyn Thurman Butler.

Table of Contents

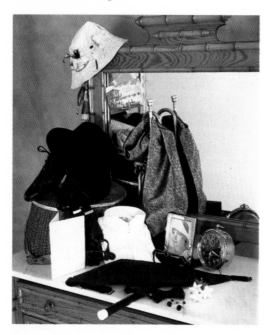

Photo: Courtesy House of Bianchi and Modern Bride

Chapter 1
Everything in Season

"Will you marry me?"

"Yes!"

In this day and age, either you or your fiance could have asked that question. Whether it happened during a romantic dinner, while skiing down a mountain, or during the Super Bowl, you both said the timeless, "Yes!" And now you are ready to plan your wedding.

A million decisions face you. When and where are only the beginning. Who will be your attendants, who will be his? What will you both wear? How formal do you want the ceremony to be? What about the reception? Where will you go for your honeymoon? Where will you live? How will you furnish your new home?

How do you make all these decisions? Where do you start?

Let's Start with Color

In the last twenty years, the seasonal color theory has revolutionized the way people dress and organize their wardrobe, makeup, and furnishings. Carole Jackson's 1980 bestseller, *Color Me Beautiful* (Acropolis), helped millions discover their color season. Long before she popularized the seasonal color theory, however, Suzanne Caygill, founder of the Academy of Color in San Francisco, had been doing color analysis by the seasons. And Gerri Pinckney and Marge Swenson, who taught Carole Jackson at their Fashion Academy of Costa Mesa, have been working with seasonal colors since 1972. Their book, *New Image for Women* (Acropolis Books, 1987), has contributed much to the practical applications of the theory. Of course, artist and colorist Johannes Itten of the famous Bauhaus School is credited with originating the idea, and it was he who noticed that his best students seemed to paint with colors that complemented their own physical coloring.

If "color fever" happened long before you were born and you have missed discovering whether you are a dramatic Winter, a classic Summer, a romantic Spring, or a natural Autumn, it's time you did. And, if you think white is the only color you need be concerned with, what about the flowers, the bridesmaids' dresses, and your trousseau?

Color can help you plan every aspect of this most exciting event of your life—from your engagement ring to your wedding dress, makeup, and hair style; from your attendants' dresses to the flowers for the reception; from your bridal gifts to your first home furnishings. Color is the common denominator that will help you put it all together.

Let's make sure you know your color season . . . and your groom's too, for that matter.

Winter? Summer? Spring? Autumn?

All proponents of the seasonal color theory agree on two basic premises. First, your skin has either cool or warm undertones. Winters and Summers have cool undertones, due to the predominance of blue pigment in their skin. Springs and Autumns have warm undertones because their skin has more yellow pigmentation. Second, cool colors complement skin with cool, blue undertones. But skin with warm, yellow undertones glows in colors with the same warm characteristics.

Look at your own skin, hair, and eye coloring. Winters are dramatic, with high contrasts between skin, hair, and eyes. Their skin color ranges from white to beige to olive to brown. Their eyes are usually dark, but can also be gray-blue, gray-green, or even hazel. Winters usually have dark hair that ranges from brown to black with blue undertones.

Summers are soft and gentle, with skin color ranging from light beige to beige with light pink to very pink cheeks. Summers have ash blonde or light ash brown hair. Their eyes are a grayed blue, green, or hazel.

Autumns are earthy naturals. Their skin ranges from ivory to peach to deep golden beige or brown, and their hair has warm highlights, varying from red to red-brown to golden-brown to charcoal black. Autumn eyes are most often green or brown.

Springs are light and bright. Their hair is usually flaxen, strawberry blonde, or golden-brown. Their eyes are very clear blue, green, aqua, or amber; skin can be ivory, peach, peach beige, or peach pink.

Winters sparkle in icy colors, jewel-tones, black and white. Summers glimmer in soft neutrals, pastels, and dusty mid-tones. Autumns glow in muted mid-tones, ivories, and earth tones. Springs are radiant in light but bright colors.

If you are having trouble deciding whether you are a cool or a warm-skinned person, a professional color consultant can offer you the most reliable help. You can order a free list of excellent color analysts, trained by Lauren Smith Inc. by sending me the coupon in back of this book. Or look in the classified section of your phone book under "Color Consultants," and do some telephone interviewing. Your chosen consultant will have the experience and the draping materials to give you the most reliable analysis. The $50 to $100 and two hours you spend with one of these trained consultants will save you time and money, not just on your wedding, but on your wardrobe and home furnishings for the rest of your life.

Find Your Own Season

Not everyone can get to a color consultant. Here is how to do your own color evaluation. This test is excerpted from my earlier book, *Your Colors at Home* (Acropolis Books, 1985). This guide to decorating with your seasonal colors will also be invaluable in helping you put the results of this test to work in your wedding and your home.

You'll need three things for this test:

1. A mirror

2. Daylight

3. The tests on the next few pages.

Set the mirror up by a window so you can study your skin closely. No makeup allowed; you are looking for the undertones, the basic hue that lies beneath the surface of the skin. It may not be easy for you to see, especially if you're not accustomed to working with the subtleties of color. Carole Jackson of *Color Me Beautiful* suggests that if you can't determine your skin's undertones by studying your face, you should examine your wrist by holding it over a very white piece of paper. If you're still not sure, check the rest of your body, especially the parts you hide beneath a bathing suit, which never get tanned, she says. Those areas retain the skin tones that are really *you,* the ones by which you can truly judge your color category, or season.

Sometimes it helps to study the varieties of "whites" offered on most paint charts. Ivory (or antique white or candlelight white) leans toward yellow, and icy white (or bright white or cool white) has blue undertones. Visit a good paint store and bring home a color card or a range of color chips of whites. You'll easily see the difference. And, it can help you see the difference in your own skin's undertones.

Winter Color Clues

Most of us are Winters. We have blue, or cool, undertones to our skins, which means we sparkle in colors that have the same cool, basic hues.

If you're a Winter, the basic color of your skin will be one of the following:

- White
- Light-to-dark taupe-beige
- Light-to-dark rose-beige
- Light-to-dark olive
- Light-to-dark taupe-brown
- Light-to-dark rose-brown
- Light-to-dark olive-brown
- Black

Your eyes are likely to be:

- Light-to-dark brown
- Brown-black
- Gray-blue
- Violet-blue
- Gray-green
- Yellow-green

- Turquoise

- Hazel (gray-brown with green or blue)

Your hair will be one of these colors (only your natural color counts):

- Black

- Brown-black

- Medium-to-dark ash brown

- Medium brown with red highlights

- Silver-gray

Because Winters do vary so much, it may be difficult for you to pick this category at first glance. When in doubt, open your closet door and study the clothes you've acquired. If two thirds of your wardrobe is in vivid colors that have a blue base, then without doubt, you're a Winter like recent brides Demi Moore and Maria Shriver.

Summer Color Clues

Summers have the same cool, blue undertones to their skins as Winters. But where a Winter's skin could be white, taupe-beige, light-to-dark rose-beige, olive, brown or black, a Summer's will be softer: light beige, light beige with pink, very pink, or light-to-medium pink-beige.

Although the undertones of a Summer's skin are always blue, its color will be one of the following:

- Light beige

- Light beige with pink cheeks

- Very pink

- Light-to-medium pink beige

A Summer's eyes will be:

- Blue
- Gray-blue
- Green
- Gray-green
- Light gray
- Aqua
- Hazel (blue or green with brown)
- Light brown

If your natural hair color is listed below, you are likely to be a Summer:

- Light-to-medium ash blonde
- Light-to-dark ash brown
- Medium brown with auburn highlights
- Ash-gray

If you are vacillating between Winter and Summer, check your eyes out carefully. Medium or dark brown eyes, or eyes that are brown-black definitely tip the vote to Winter. Eyes that are blue or gray-blue, green or gray-green, aqua, light gray, hazel, or light brown may peg you as a Summer like recent bride Caroline Kennedy.

Autumn Color Clues

Once again, Nature calls the color shots: Autumns personify their season with coloring based on rich, yellow undertones, often crowned with glowing reds.

An Autumn's skin tones are best described as:

- Ivory
- Beige ivory

- Light-to-dark peach
- Light-to-dark golden beige
- Light-to-dark golden brown

If you're an Autumn, your eyes are likely to be:

- Light-to-dark brown
- Golden brown
- Gold-green
- Jade green
- Turquoise
- Hazel (golden brown with green)

These hair colors are pretty predictable on an Autumn:

- Red
- Copper
- Chestnut
- Medium-to-dark golden blonde
- Medium-to-dark golden brown
- Charcoal black
- Golden gray

Although there are fewer Autumns, you'll find some well-knowns in this category like exuberant bride Fergi and actress Molly Ringwald.

Spring Color Clues

Like Autumns, Springs are characterized by warm—or yellow—undertones to their skin. The easiest way to isolate a Spring is to think of Spring itself. It's the season that brings forth the clearest, brightest colors of the year. And when it comes to seasonal color categories, Springs follow suit, with the most delicate complexions and the brightest, clearest eye colors.

A Spring's skin can be any of these:

- Ivory
- Peach-ivory
- Peach
- Peach-pink
- Light-to-medium peach-beige

Eyes fall into the following categories:

- Blue
- Green
- Aqua
- Amber
- Light brown

If you are a Spring, your hair is likely to be a natural:

- Light-to-medium flaxen blonde
- Strawberry blonde
- Auburn
- Light-to-medium golden brown
- Pearl gray

Some well-known Springs are Christie Brinkley, Darryl Hannah, Sissy Spacek, and Vanessa Williams.

Find Your Best Colors

Winters are best in the true and primary colors, as well as their darker, bluer shades. Think *true, blue,* and *vivid.* The very fair Winter is most flattered by the icy or deep colors; the Winter with darker skin is better in brighter colors. Winters should avoid any color with a yellow undertone. Brown is another no-no unless it's dark enough to look almost black. Winter is the only season that looks good in pure white or black.

Summers are best in pastels and soft neutrals. Think *blue, pink,* and *soft.* The very fair blonde Summer is complemented by light colors; brunette Summers are better in the deeper shades of their palette. Summers should avoid pure white, black, or any color with a yellow undertone.

Autumns are best in the rich colors of fall. Think *earthy, yellow,* and *intense.* The very fair Autumn is better in the more muted shades; the Autumn with darker skin looks better in the brighter colors of her palette, too drab in earth tones. Autumns should avoid pure white, black, navy, gray, pink, and any color with a blue undertone.

Springs are best in crisp colors. Think *clear, yellow,* and *bright.* The very fair Spring can be overwhelmed by bright colors; the Spring with more definite coloring is better in bright colors, too pale in light colors. Springs should avoid pure white, black, and any color with a blue undertone.

The Winter Bride

Cool, self-assured, and sophisticated, the Winter bride is often a dramatic with high cheekbones, prominent features, and an angular build. Her skin, with its blue undertones, ranges from white to beige to olive to brown to black. Her eyes are usually dark, but can also be gray-blue, green, or even hazel. Winters have dark hair that varies from brown to black.

Whether she's married in a cathedral, hotel ballroom, or starlit roof, the dramatic Winter wears high fashion with a flourish. She'll sparkle in a sophisticated bridal sheath of white satin, brocade, or velvet with the longest of trains, surrounded by her jewel tones: ruby red, sapphire blue, emerald green, royal purple, or black and white.

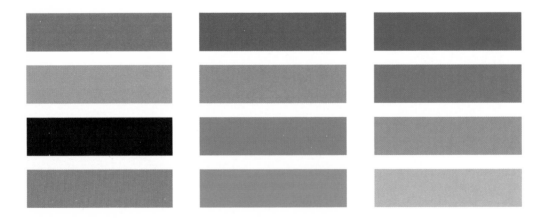

Everything in Season

The Summer Bride

Cool, calm and refined, the Summer bride is often a classic with a balanced, well-proportioned build and well-modeled features. Her skin has the same blue undertones as the Winter, but it ranges from light beige to beige with light pink to very pink blushing cheeks. Her coloring is light-to-medium featuring ash blonde or light ash brown hair and gray-blue, green, or hazel eyes.

Whether she's married in a church, at a country club, or in a military chapel, the classic Summer prefers the time-honored traditions. She'll look lovely in an off-white, classically styled dress of peau de soie, taffeta, or lace with long, fitted sleeves, surrounded by her pastels: powder pink, pastel yellow, mint green, powder blue, and lilac.

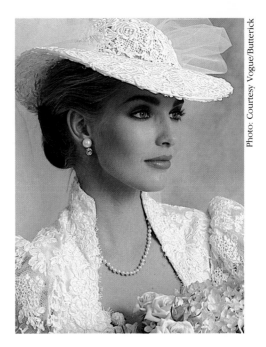

Photo: Courtesy Vogue/Butterick

Photo: Courtesy Vogue/Butterick

The Autumn Bride

Warm, friendly, and outgoing, the Autumn bride is often a natural, all-American outdoor type, with broad shoulders and slim hips. With yellow undertones, her ivory, peach, golden beige or golden brown skin, glows with health. Her eyes are brown, golden brown, gold-green, jade green, turquoise, or hazel. Her hair is fiery red, copper, chestnut, golden blonde, or brown, and can even be charcoal black.

Whether her wedding takes place before a justice of the peace, in an historic inn, or an English manor, the natural Autumn perfers simplicity. She'll wear an oyster white dress or suit in silk, linen, or wool, and glow in surroundings of the rich colors of fall: tangerine, orange, gold, turquoise, or periwinkle.

The Spring Bride

Charming, flirtatious, and feminine, the Spring bride is often a romantic with soft features and rounded figure. Her light, bright skin ranges from ivory, to peach, peach beige, or peach pink—all with yellow undertones. Her hair is flaxen, strawberry blonde, or golden-brown. Her eyes are very clear blue, green, aqua, or amber.

Whether her wedding is staged in a chapel, an antebellum plantation, or on a river boat, the romantic Spring combines high fashion with femininity. She'll wear a full-skirted dress of ivory organza, taffeta, or tulle, trimmed with ruffles and lace, surrounded by Spring's clear colors: warm pink, peach, aqua, yellow, green or periwinkle.

Photo: Courtesy Vogue/Butterick

Len Price

Dawn for Bethann Management

Hair and Makeup: L'Oreal
Stylist: Joe McDevitt

Everything in Season

Makeup for Your Wedding Day

The Dramatic Bride

Dawn is a dramatic bride with a self-assured, sophisticated style. Her sparkling dark eyes and hair look even more vivid when complemented by L'Oreal's Visuelle Invisible Coverage Makeup (Sand Beige), Pressed Powder (Medium), and balanced by Creme Rich lipstick in daring plum tones. Her blush is rich Plume. Her eyes dance with black lashes, strikingly accented by L'Oreal's gray-toned Couleur Couleur shadows.

Dawn is the dramatic who dares to be a little bolder. Her makeup emphasizes her eyes and lips.

To create an even more vivid contrast between her skin and hair, Dawn used Performing Preference Dark Brown Haircolor by L'Oreal. It brought out her rich natural highlights while leaving her hair lustrous and well conditioned. Before putting her hair up, she applied Studio Line Styling Gel to keep a very neat sleek look.

Hair and Makeup by L'Oreal
Illustrations by Craig Avner

Before

After

Len Price

Holly for Click

Hair and Makeup: L'Oreal
Stylist: Joe McDevitt

Everything in Season

Makeup for Your Wedding Day

The Classic Bride

Holly is a classic, cool skinned, fair-haired bride whose elegance defies time. Her well modeled features are enhanced with L'Oreal's Mattique Illuminating Matte Makeup (Soft Ivory), Tulipe blush, and Visuelle Pressed Powder (Light). L'Oreal's Lash-Out Mascara in Black was used to elongate her lashes while her shadow is in their plum tones. Her lipstick is deep rosy plum.

Holly is refined and understated in every way. Her makeup projects a balanced, assured look.

To set off her eyes, Holly decided to add subtle highlights to her hair, creating a halo around her face. She chose the blonde shade of Brush-On Soft Color Highlights. She used Studio Line Directional Styling Spray on the sides for extra lift, while keeping the natural movement of her hair.

Hair and Makeup by L'Oreal
Illustrations by Craig Avner

Before

After

Colors for Brides

Len Prince

Gisela for Click

Hair and Makeup: L'Oreal
Stylist: Joe McDevitt

Makeup for Your Wedding Day

The Natural Bride

Gisella is a warm natural beauty, healthy and a little wild. Her sun-kissed skin is enhanced with L'Oreal's Mattique Illuminating Matte Makeup (Golden Bisque), dusted with Visuelle Pressed Powder (Medium). Her cheeks glow with Capucine blush, and her eyes are veiled with black/brown lashes and shadowed in Couleur Couleur golden brown. Her Creme Riche lipstick is a generous earth tone.

Gisella is a natural earthy bride. Her makeup emphasizes her lovely eyes and warm glow of health.

To enrich and highlight her natural brown hair, Gisella applied Avantage Auburn, a semipermanent, peroxide/ammonia-free haircolor. She accents and defines her natural curls with Studio Line Pumping Curls and holds her contained yet wild mane with a Studio Line weightless styling spray.

Hair and Makeup by L'Oreal
Illustrations by Craig Avner

Before

After

Len Price

Susanne for Click

Hair and Makeup: L'Oreal
Stylist: Joe McDevitt

Everything in Season

Makeup for Your Wedding Day

The Romantic Bride

Susanne is a romantic bride with her fair hair, warm skin, and softly rounded features. Her charming, feminine look is complemented by L'Oreal's Visuelle Invisible Coverage Makeup (Ivory) and Peony blush, dusted with Visuelle Pressed Powder (Light). Her lashes are brushed with Lash Out Lash Extending Black/Brown Mascara and her eyes shadowed in shell pink tones. Her lipstick is a warm pink.

Susanne with her long wavy hair is alluring but innocent. Her makeup is bright, fresh, and delicate.

To accentuate her Romantic look, Susanne decided to color her natural light brown hair with Excellence Soft and Natural in a Reddish Blonde shade. Full of body and manageability, her hair's lustrous reddish tones complete her warm, romantic image.

Hair and Makeup by L'Oreal
Illustrations by Craig Avner

Before

After

Find Your Own Style

Your wedding is your day to star. Though you'll need to consider your groom's and attendants' color seasons, when in doubt go with the colors that make *you* look your very best.

In my years of design and consulting, I've discovered there's much more to the color seasons than what colors are most flattering. Your color season may also tell you something about your clothing personality and the way you look at life.

Your personal fashion style reflects the way you like to dress as well as the way you are shaped. Many studies emphasize body proportions alone as a basis for clothing selection, completely ignoring your personality. But I believe that dressing to type is in many ways more valid than dressing to proportion. In fact, your personality may actually be affected by your body proportions.

Personal style is unique to every woman, but it really comes down to two types:

- the woman who has a more easygoing attitude toward life, reflected in her casual approach to makeup, hair, and clothing; and,

- the woman who likes a more finished look in makeup, hair, and clothing.

While these two types may look very different, they are really not opposites. It's just a matter of degree: more or less. As a rule, Winters and Summers are more formal; Autumns and Springs, less formal. This attitude is reflected in the way they dress and the way they decorate. Women who appreciate formality do so with drama or tradition. Less formal women tend to be romantic or natural. Here are more complete descriptions of these personality types. You'll see how color can even affect your personality and approach to life.

Dramatics

The woman with a dramatic personality is usually five feet five inches or taller with an angular build. Her high cheekbones and prominent features, dark vivid coloring and self-assured, sophisticated manner, make her a stand-out in any crowd. She is formal and dignified, preferring sleek hair, worn up or sweeping her shoulders. Dramatics are frequently Winters or dark Autumns. The Dramatic delights in fashion extremes that emphasize her flamboyant features.

Classics

The classic personality is usually five feet three inches to five feet six inches with a balanced, well-proportioned build and well-modeled features. Her coloring is light-to-medium and she wears her hair in simple, but soft styles. Her overall manner is poised, refined, ladylike, and well mannered. Classics are usually Summers. The classic avoids all extremes of fashion, preferring the time-honored traditionals.

Naturals

Naturals are ordinarily five feet five inches and more, with broad shoulders, the all-American outdoor type. Her features are somewhat angular in a long or broad face. Her coloring is natural and earthy, her hair casual, unset or windblown. Her manner is friendly, relaxed, open, and frank. Naturals are often Autumns, and prefer simplicity and comfort in their dress.

Romantics

The romantic is five feet three inches to five feet six inches with a rounded, feminine figure and beautiful features. Her coloring is striking and she wears her hair in a softly curled style. Her general manner is flirtatious, charmingly feminine but softly sophisticated. Romantics are often Springs, but can also be Winters. They combine high fashion with soft femininity.

Composites

If you are certain of your clothing personality, be grateful. You have an advantage. Many of us are a little of one and a little of another. For instance, you might have the coloring of a Classic but the body proportions and earthy wit of a Natural. Or, you could have the sharp contrasting coloring of a Dramatic but the soft features and feminine figure of the Romantic. A consultant can help you define your style and advise you on the best styles for your complicated fashion personality.

How Formal Are You?

As you decide how formal you want your wedding to be, remember: you are the star, so always start with your personal style and your dress. If you have been lucky enough to inherit a beautiful wedding dress from an ancestor, close relative or friend, then its formality should determine how elaborate the wedding is. Otherwise, it is up to you, your fiance, and your wedding budget.

Now think about your personal style and how it fits into one of these four wedding categories:

Ultraformal. These elaborate events are almost always held in a church or synagogue in the evening or late afternoon, although an ultraformal Catholic wedding takes place with mass at noon. You would have six to twelve attendants, one or two flower girls, a ring bearer and train bearer, 200 or more guests, and an elegant dinner or buffet reception, dancing, the works. This is the wedding for a dramatic personality.

Formal. A formal wedding is most frequently held in a house of worship but can also take place at a private club, a home, the ballroom of a hotel, or even a garden. With four to six attendants and 100 to 200 guests, it is a little less formal. It is ordinarily scheduled for late afternoon or evening, except for the noon Catholic mass. This more sedate wedding is for the traditional, classic bride.

Semiformal. Except that it is not tied to formal rules and can be a less elaborately decorated and conducted event, the semiformal wedding may be held in any of the places where an ultraformal or formal wedding is held. You could have fewer attendants and a simpler reception, or twelve attendants and a full-of-flowers romantic reception. Romantic, adventurous people who like everything their own way, with no one telling them how it has been done in the past, should create their own semiformal wedding.

Informal. Informal weddings may be held before a magistrate or before a small group of friends with your family clergy in attendance. It may take place at any time during the morning or afternoon, usually not in the evening. You would have a maid or matron of honor and a best man. No-fuss, practical people who want everything to be natural and fun should go for the informal wedding.

What to Wear?

Generally, a floor-length white gown of satin, peau de soie, faille, silk, lace, velvet (except in the summer), taffeta, chiffon, tulle, or organza with long sleeves or long gloves and a long train, complementary veil covering the train or extending to train-length would be appropriate only for ultraformal or formal ceremonies. A simpler, floor-length or shorter white or pastel dress with an elbow-length or short veil is perfect for a semiformal wedding. A street-length dress or suit, hat, and gloves are all you need for an informal ceremony.

If you are not sure what your personal wedding style is, take this little quiz.

1. You are given the opportunity to try on any of the following designer outfits. Which would you choose?

A. An almost backless black satin evening dress.

B. An elegant silk dinner dress with a fitted jacket.

C. A floral print dress with a colorful cotton sash.

D. Perfectly-fitted jeans and a fringed shirt.

2. Which would you choose for your dream home?

A. A luxurious estate with views of the sea and mountains and a long driveway lined with columnar trees and formal flower beds.

B. A sophisticated duplex apartment in the city, filled with objets d'art.

C. A charming country house covered with roses, and surrounded by gardens of vegetables, herbs and flowering perennials.

D. A large, rambling house in the suburbs surrounded by tall trees and laughing children.

3. Which of the following parties would you relish an invitation to?

A. A diplomatic reception for 300.

B. The opening night reception for the local ballet company.

C. A dinner party for eight at friends'.

D. A picnic and softball game.

4. You win the lottery and are given twenty minutes to pack a bag and catch transportation to . . .

A. A tour of the French chateaux with an extravagant evening party at each.

B. A museum tour of Washington, D.C.

C. A riverboat trip down the Mississippi to visit old Civil War mansions.

D. A camping trip in Yellowstone National Park.

5. Which form of transportation would you choose if given the time to travel in style?

A. A private jet.

B. An elegant Jaguar.

C. A cruise ship.

D. A bicycle.

Interpreting the Quiz

This quiz is pretty easy to interpret. If you chose mostly A's, your wedding should be ultraformal. If your answers were predominantly B's, you are a formal personality. With C's you are semiformal, and with D's informal.

You'll learn more about what goes into each kind of wedding in the chapters to follow. Now that you know your color season and your personal style, let's move on with your plans.

Chapter 2
The Ring and the Rituals

Marriage

Every year more than 5 million people are married in the United States, promising to love and honor each other for a lifetime. No matter what is happening in the world at large, marriage is still the basis for family life, as it has been for most of the history of mankind.

Needless to say, during that long, long history, many traditions have developed. White, a symbol of purity, is the traditional color for bridal dresses in western cultures. Of course we all know that the bride must also wear "something old, something new, something borrowed, and something blue." The old is her link with the past, the new the hope of the future, the borrowed is a tie to friendship, and the blue symbolizes faithfulness. Nelly Custis, George Washington's adopted daughter, is said to have begun the tradition in this country of wearing a bridal veil when she covered her hair with a lovely scarf in 1799; but Roman brides really began the custom more than 2,000 years ago. The veil in their day was supposed to ward off evil spirits and symbolize the bride's chastity.

The wedding kiss began back with the Romans, too. The kiss was actually the legal bond between a man and woman. During a special betrothal ceremony, they kissed, joined right hands, and were legally bonded. After this kiss, if either one died, the other was officially entitled to the wedding presents. In the early days of Christianity the kiss became part of the marriage ceremony.

Somehow, it seems everyone attending a wedding is in love. Look around at the misty-eyed couples of all ages, smiling fondly at each other.

What more appropriate time for the bride to toss her bouquet to the unmarried women and the groom to throw the newly extracted garter to the unmarried men? The next couple to be married could be these best catchers, who knows? This custom is said to have started in medieval France.

Wedding guests throw rice at the departing couple as they race off on their honeymoon because rice was once the symbol of fertility and long life. Now rice is often replaced by birdseed or pot pourri because uncooked rice has proved harmful to birds who may still feast on it long after the wedding party departs.

The Ring

One of the oldest traditions to have come down through the ages is the presentation of wedding rings. The eternity of love is symbolized in the circular shape of the ring; the ring therefore unites the couple forever. The third finger of the left hand became the "ring finger" because people once believed that there was a vein in this finger running directly to the heart.

Shopping for your rings and deciding whether or not you want a double ring ceremony may be one of your first consumer decisions together. In the double ring ceremony, the bride and groom exchange rings with each other. Otherwise, only the bride receives a wedding band. It's a choice that's up to the two of you.

Gold is the traditional metal for wedding rings, but the warm tones of yellow gold are best for Autumns and Springs. Cool white metals—platinum, white gold, and silver—harmonize with the Winter and Summer palettes. Gold is measured in karats with 24 karats being its purest form. Alloys are frequently mixed with the gold to strengthen it. But the more alloys mixed in, the fewer the karats of gold. For example, a 14-karat gold ring contains 10 karats of alloys. Yellow gold can have copper and silver alloys. White gold has nickel, zinc, and copper alloys. Green-tinted gold has silver, copper, and zinc; and pink gold has copper. Platinum is a shimmery white metal and is considered the strongest ring metal. You'll be wearing this ring for a long, long time, so base your decision not only on the metal's contents, but on the most "harmonious" tone for your coloring.

Your seasonal color palette offers many more choices for your engagement ring, if you are lucky enough to receive one. This ring represents a large investment for your fiance, and he may want to surprise you with it when he "pops" the question, at an engagement party or another romantic moment. If you can, discreetly anticipate his selection of the gemstone by suggesting the types of stones and metals that are in tune with your palette. Or better yet, choose the ring together as the first symbol of your commitment to each other. Make sure that your engagement ring and your wedding ring match, if you plan to wear them both on the same hand.

The American Gem Society (AGS) recommends guiding your selection of a gem on the four c's: *cut, color, clarity,* and *carat weight.* Gemstones like opals are smoothly cut, and are called *cabochons.* Most stones are carved or *faceted,* however, to reflect light and sparkle. They can be cut in square or rectangular shapes, round, oval, pear-shaped or marquise which is oval with pointed ends. Each kind of gemstone varies in color. The most valuable diamonds have no color, but the most expensive rubies will be pinkish red, deep blue for sapphires, deep green for emeralds. The bluer the better for aquamarines. Flaws affect the *clarity* of a gemstone and its value. Gemstones are measured in *carats.* Generally, the more carats the more valuable is the stone; but the color, clarity, and cut must also be good in the finest gemstones.

The American Gem Society recommends choosing the stone first, then the setting. Be a careful shopper. Consult a knowledgeable jeweler who is a member of the AGS. In AGS stores you'll see the titles, "Registered Jeweler" and "Certified Gemologist," signifying that the jeweler has met AGS standards of professionalism and business conduct and that you can trust him to guide your selection and purchase. Much of the following information about gem quality and history comes from American Gem Society publications. Their address is listed at the back of this book. Check with your insurance agent, too, so that you can insure both wedding and engagement rings as soon as they are purchased.

Choosing a Diamond

Cutting of a diamond takes supreme skill. If the cut is too shallow or too deep, it will not sparkle. The sparkle comes from the prismatic facets cut into the stone. The well-cut round diamond should have 58 exactly placed facets to allow light entering to bounce back and not "leak" out. Common cuts for diamonds are round or "brilliant;" oval, oval with pointed top and bottom or "marquise;" pear-shaped or "teardrop;" heart-shaped; and the rectangular "emerald" cut. The multi-pointed starburst is a new sophisticated choice for the most dramatic Winters.

As we said, the finest quality diamonds have no color at all. The AGS rates a diamond's color from 0 for "colorless" to 10 for "yellow." The more yellow in the body color, or interior, of the diamond, the less value it has. Any internal or external "flaw" on a diamond restricts the passage of light and materially reduces its value. Look for a stone with clarity or no flaws when magnified ten times.

Carat weight is the fourth factor in determining the value of your stone, but it is not as important as cut, color, and clarity. You may even opt for a diamond of fewer carats that's worth more than a larger one because the cut, color, and clarity are finer. It takes skill, knowledge and experience to choose a diamond. Your jeweler should give you a written guarantee and a certificate of registration proving the diamond's value for insurance purposes. This appraisal will have to be updated every five years.

The Diamond Information Center cautions that diamonds can scratch other jewelry, so keep that in mind when you wear it with other rings or take it off to put it in the jewelry box. And, they recommend taking your diamond off while participating in sports. Surprisingly, you might chip it. Once a year have your diamond professionally cleaned by your jeweler and the setting checked for loose prongs.

Winter's Sparkling Gemstones

Seventy-five percent of brides receive diamonds, but they are not every girl's best friend. Diamonds are indeed the sparkling stone for dramatic Winters and adventurous Springs. They were first set into rings in 1477 when Maximilian of Austria gave Mary of Burgundy a diamond solitaire to celebrate their engagement, but they were reserved for the rich and noble until the nineteenth century. Now, with a little smart shopping, diamonds are affordable for many young couples. A very small, ¼ carat stone in a modest setting can cost as much as $500 or more; ½ carat about $1,000 and one carat about $2,500 or more.

Winters also sparkle in emeralds, rubies, and sapphires. Cut, color, clarity, and carat weight determine the value of these exquisite stones also. Check all of them when you purchase these highly prized gemstones.

The vivid green of emeralds is said to symbolize faithfulness and the Romans dedicated this beautiful stone to Venus, goddess of love. They believed that emeralds improved your intelligence and gave you the power to predict the future. The Spaniards took every emerald they could find when they conquered the Incas in the 16th century. Even today, Colombia, South America, is the source of the finest emeralds. The rectangular step-cut, known as the emerald cut in other gemstones as well, is the most popular because it shows off the emerald's brilliant green color.

Sapphires come in a rainbow of colors, ranging from pale gray to pinkish-orange. The name comes from the Greek word for blue, *sappheiros,* and the most valuable are rich, bright blue. The Persians believed that the earth rests on a giant sapphire and this beautiful stone was considered a symbol of truth and constancy. The Kashmir region in India was the traditional source of the finest sapphires, but today they are mined in Montana, Australia, Africa, Sri Lanka, Burma, and Thailand. Star sapphires were believed to protect against witchcraft by the Singhalese. Numerous needle-like inclusions make sapphires translucent. When oriented properly, light is reflected in a star-like sparkle that seems to float across the stone. A dome-shaped cut reveals the star which is not visible in the emerald-cut or faceted stones.

The clear red ruby has always been worn by kings as a symbol of divine power. Actually, both sapphires and rubies are varieties of the mineral corundum, with red rubies on one end of the scale and plum and pink sapphires on the other. And, like their sapphire cousin, rubies can have a luminous star, but must be cut in the dome shape to display it to advantage. Fine, large rubies are very rare and may be worth more than diamonds of a similar size because they are still mined by careful sifting and panning, much as they were hundreds of years ago.

Winters should not forget beautiful white pearls set in platinum with diamonds or even the rarer black pearls when choosing a ring. Whether natural or cultured, pearls are especially appropriate for the bride with the classic clothing personality.

Glimmers for Summers

Summer's gems are softer in color and more muted in tone. Pink, light blue, or plum sapphires are more harmonious than the bright blue kashmir stone. Rare pink pearls, rather than white or yellowish ones, are a Summer treasure. Pearls are perfect for classic beauties, in round, egg, teardrop, or pear shapes. The Romans prized them so much that women wore them to bed with their lovers. The rich creaminess of pearls improves with body heat. In Europe they have been the rage since the Crusaders first brought them home to their loves.

Opals, called by Shakespeare "the queen of gems," are for Summer brides. The mysterious opal was a Roman symbol of hope because of the rainbow they believed was locked inside. This play of color comes from diffraction of light in the layers of silica spheres that make up opals. Black opals are the most valuable. Their dark background color dances with flashes of other colors, but because they are not pure black, can be worn by the most adventurous Summers and all Winters. More pastel in feeling are white opals, crystal opals, and water opals. Opals are usually cut in the dome shape to show off their many colors. Their quality is judged on the number of colors they display and the evenness of the pattern.

Summer's royal gemstone is the amethyst, a variety of quartz that can vary from transparent light purple to dark, rich burgundy. It is said that one day when Bacchus, the god of wine, was feeling testy, he swore that he would have tigers eat the first mortal who crossed his path. The maiden Amethyst was the unlucky person, but was saved by the goddess Diana who turned her to stone before the tigers could get there. Bacchus repented and poured wine over the stone, turning it purple. Roman women believed the amethyst would keep their husbands faithful. Amethysts are readily available and quite modestly priced. They can be faceted to sparkle.

Autumn's Glow

Autumns may also reign in dark purple or ripe plum-colored amethysts. Their ruby is the very deepest, darkest red. Their pearls are the color of rich cream; their emeralds the golden-green of harvest. The fire opal with its yellows, oranges, reds, and browns should be reserved strictly for Autumns.

The golden topaz is a special treat for Autumns, from the reddish-brown sherry topaz to the blistering Imperial. In ancient times it was believed that the topaz made its wearer stronger, smarter, more even tempered, and happier. This handsome stone is one of the most durable, resists scratching, and retains a high polish. It does chip, though, just like a diamond.

The garnet is another rainbow-filled gem. It follows the spectrum from red to green—but never blue. The most popular garnets are the deep violet-red almandine, the red-orange pyrope, and the light plum rhodolite. Spessartite garnets range from tangerine to cinnamon in color. The rarest is the emerald green and radite. Garnets can be dome cut or faceted.

Spring's Fantasies

Because of its clarity and its warm greenish blue, the aquamarine is Spring's very own emerald. The aquamarine is said to bring happiness and everlasting youth to the wearer. They can be cut into a variety of shapes, are easily available, and affordable. Step-cut, they are most brilliant.

Springs will enjoy happiness in marriage if they choose the new grass green of the peridot for their engagement ring. This unusual gemstone was called the "gem of the sun" by the ancient Egyptians and believed to be invisible by night. They are very affordable and plentiful and can be faceted into the emerald or brilliant cuttings to send sparks flying. In greens that range from light yellow-green to intense bright green, the peridot is ideal for Springs.

A really daring Spring may want to flaunt a rare pink topaz. It is the most valuable of all the topazes and is said to give courage and energy to the wearer—just what you need for your wedding day. The lighter lavender amethyst will also complement amber-eyed Springs, as will creamy pearls, set in gold and surrounded by diamonds.

Brilliant   Oval   Emerald   Pear   Marquise   Heart Shape

Antiques

For the more unusual settings, antiques offer all brides something special—history as well as beauty. Be sure to buy from a reputable jeweler known for antique jewels. They must be at least 100 years old to qualify as antiques. You should be able to find the ring's signage, a marking inscribed into the piece that tells how many karats of gold, the year, and city in which it was assayed as well as the jeweler's mark.

If you are fortunate enough to have inherited a family heirloom, there are several things you should do. Have the ring reappraised and insured; have a jeweler take a look at the setting, as it may be old and fragile and need new prongs. Then, as the latest recipient of this prized possession, you must decide whether to wear it "as is," or whether to use the stone or stones in a more appropriate setting, or one that better suits your seasonal palette. Talk to a trusted jeweler and look at the many settings—both antique and not-so-antique—to find out which fits your personality.

Jewels for Every Season

	Winter	Summers	Autumns	Springs
Metals	Platinum	Platinum	Yellow gold	Yellow gold
	White gold	White gold Pink gold	Green-tinted gold	
	Silver	Silver	—	—
Gems	Diamond	—	—	Diamond
	Emerald	—	Golden-green emerald	Light yellow- green emerald
	Sapphire	Pink, plum, or light-blue sap- phire	—	Yellow sap- phire
	Black opal	Black, white, crystal, or water opal	Fire opal	Crystal opal
	White pearls Black pearls	Pink pearls	Cream pearls	Cream pearls
	—	Amethyst	Burgundy amethyst	Lavender amethyst
	Clear, red ruby	Plum and pink ruby	Deepest red ruby	Pink ruby
	—	Blue topaz	Golden topaz	Yellow topaz
	—	Garnet	Garnet	Yellow-orange garnet
	—	—	Olive Peridot	Peridot
	—	Blue Aqua- marine	—	Aquamarine

Chapter 3
A Wedding Checklist

Setting the Date

You have fallen in love, you know what your colors and your style are, and now you are ready to set the date. First, consult your parents and your fiance's family. His parents should call or write to your parents to arrange an informal occasion to meet, if they have not already done so. Together all of you can plan the best time to have the ceremony.

Unless you just can't wait, give yourself plenty of time—at least six months, preferably a year, to plan the wedding just the way you want it. Consider scheduling it during your season. That way the clothes in the stores and the flowers at the florists will be in your colors. In fact, all of nature will be ready to complement your special day.

Often, churches and reception spots are booked a year ahead. Before you set yourself up for disappointment, give these places a call—if only a preliminary one—so that you don't plan your dream wedding on an impossible date or place.

Who Pays for What

Speaking of playing a part, let's discuss who pays for which parts. Traditionally, your parents are responsible for the expenses of the ceremony and the reception afterwards, including the invitations and announcements, the flowers, the church or synagogue staff (the organist, sexton, and soloist), your bridal dress and trousseau, the photographer, the wedding cake, transportation to the church and reception, help, music, food, and drinks served at the reception. They may also want to retain a wedding consultant and pay for your attendants' dresses. And, they will want to give you and your bridegroom a special wedding gift.

If you have no family, if this is your second marriage, or if you are mature enough to take on the wedding yourself, these will be your responsibilities. In addition, you should pay for a gift for your future husband and your attendants, your own medical checkup, and your bridegroom's ring if you are having a double-ring ceremony.

Your fiance should pay for your engagement and wedding rings, the marriage license, gifts for you and his best man and ushers as well as their gloves, ties and boutonnieres, the bachelor dinner, and the contribution to the clergy. He should also supply the car to take the two of you away and pay for the honeymoon. His family may host the rehearsal dinner before the wedding. You could even schedule this the night before the rehearsal, if you don't want to be up late the night before the wedding. This can be nearly impossible though, if like many women, your friends and family are traveling from afar and can't be there until the night before.

There is no doubt that weddings can be very expensive. Know your limits and those of all the participants. Now is the time to establish a budget.

Here is a checklist from the Association of Bridal Consultants of who pays for what:

Bride

- ☐ Bridegroom's wedding ring
- ☐ Wedding gift for the bridegroom
- ☐ Presents for her attendants
- ☐ Housing for out-of-town attendants
- ☐ Her medical examination
- ☐ Her hair stylist and makeup artist
- ☐ A party for the bridesmaids, if no one else pays for it
- ☐ Stationery for personal notes and thank-yous
- ☐ Wedding gift book
- ☐ Wedding guest book

Bride's Family

- [ ] Bride's wedding clothes and trousseau
- [ ] Invitations, announcements, and enclosures
- [ ] Engagement and wedding photographs
- [ ] Church rental fee
- [ ] Floater insurance policy to cover wedding gifts while on display
- [ ] Fees for organist, soloist, and sexton
- [ ] Aisle carpet and canopy
- [ ] Flowers for church and reception
- [ ] Bridesmaids' bouquets
- [ ] Transportation for bridal party from house to church to reception
- [ ] Entire cost of reception
- [ ] Engagement party
- [ ] Bouquets or corsages for the bridesmaids, honor attendants, and flower girl
- [ ] Corsages given to any friends helping at the reception
- [ ] Flowers sent to any hostess entertaining for the bride or for the bride and bridegroom

Bride and/or Her Family

- [ ] Services of a bridal consultant and/or secretary
- [ ] Music for ceremony and reception
- [ ] Traffic policeman
- [ ] Security arrangements for gifts at home
- [ ] Boutonniere for the father of the bride

Bridegroom

- ☐ Marriage license
- ☐ His medical examination
- ☐ Her wedding and engagement rings
- ☐ Gift for the bride
- ☐ Bride's bouquet
- ☐ Boutonnieres for his attendants and himself
- ☐ Flowers for both mothers
- ☐ Gloves, ascots or ties for his attendants
- ☐ Housing for his out-of-town attendants
- ☐ Bachelor's dinner, if no one else pays for it
- ☐ Fee for the clergyman
- ☐ Honeymoon
- ☐ Corsage for the bride's going-away outfit
- ☐ Corsages for honored female guests, such as grandmothers or godmothers
- ☐ Shipping of wedding presents

Bridegroom's Family

- ☐ Their clothes for the wedding
- ☐ Travel and accommodations for themselves
- ☐ Wedding gift for the couple
- ☐ Rehearsal dinner

Bridesmaids

- ☐ Purchase of bridesmaids' dresses and accessories
- ☐ Transportation to and from the wedding site
- ☐ Contribution to a gift from all the bridesmaids to the bride
- ☐ An individual gift for the couple
- ☐ Shower and/or luncheon for the bride

Ushers

- ☐ Rental of wedding outfit
- ☐ Transportation to and from the wedding site
- ☐ Contribution to a gift from all the ushers to the bridegroom
- ☐ An individual gift for the couple

Out-of-town Guests

- ☐ Transportation and lodging

Here is a suggested calendar of who should schedule what, when...

	Bride	Bride and Bridegroom	Bridegroom
6—12 months	Reserve place for reception. Have your colors done by a color consultant and choose your wedding color scheme and home decorating colors. Interview and select a wedding consultant. Interview photographers, florists, musicians, caterers. Make your choices and sign the contracts. Shop for your bridal dress. Collect your attendants' sizes and shop for their dresses. Be sure both mothers are informed of your chosen color scheme and dress style. Write your engagement announcement and send with photograph to your local newspapers and that of the town where your fiance's family lives.	Decide what kind of wedding you want and where it will be held. Talk to clergyman. Reserve church or other place for ceremony. Choose your attendants. Shop for and choose your tableware, glassware, linens, other household items. Register with bridal registry at department or specialty stores. Begin your guest lists. Consult with both families.	Start honeymoon plans. Pick out engagement ring.

	Bride	Bride and Bridegroom	Bridegroom
3—6 months ahead	Select and order your invitations and announcements. Take out a floater policy with your insurance agent to cover your soon-to-arrive wedding presents. Begin addressing invitations. Shop for your trousseau. Confirm plans with caterer, photographer, musicians, florist, reception place.	Finish your guest list. Schedule medical checkups. Look for the place where you'll live. Shop for wedding ring or rings.	Consult with your fiancee and her family about your wedding attire. Arrange for yours and your attendants'. Confirm honeymoon arrangements including passports, tickets, visas. Shop for honeymoon and wedding clothes.
6 to 8 weeks	Mail invitations. Write thank you notes as gifts arrive. Have your wedding dress altered, schedule fittings for attendants' dresses. Check accessories—shoes, gloves, veil, garter, hosiery, etc. Have bridal portrait taken. Make hair and makeup appointments.	Shop for your attendants' gifts and gifts for each other. Put deposit down and reserve your new house or apartment. Renew your passports, if necessary. Make any necessary new joint financial arrangements. Apply for marriage license. Complete required religious classes, and/or other meetings. Make arrangements for bachelor's dinner and bridesmaid's luncheon. Complete seating chart and place cards for sit-down dinner.	Plan rehearsal dinner, reserve room, order food.

Colors for Brides

43

	Bride	Bride and Bridegroom	Bridegroom
One week ahead		Check details of all your plans.	
		Pack your suitcases.	
		Have fun at prenuptial parties.	
On the Big Day	Get your hair and nails done, stay calm.	Enjoy yourselves.	Check honeymoon arrangements again.
	Mail your wedding announcements to friends and newspapers.		Make sure of transportation arrangements for after the reception.
			Put clergy fee in envelope and give to best man for clergy.

Now let's get started on all these plans. It may seem as if there is a lot to do, and there is, but remember you can have fun planning your wedding. Don't make it another stressful situation. Laugh and talk and love.

Letting the World Know

Spread the good news about your impending marriage to everyone who cares about you and your fiance. Write letters and use the telephone to tell intimate friends and relatives. "A key point," says the Association of Bridal Consultants, "is to make certain all the appropriate people—close friends and relatives—are told about the same time, to avoid damaging anyone's ego."

Invite everyone to a party. It can be a brunch, a tea, a cocktail or dinner party. Invitations may be extended by telephone and followed up with a reminder a week or so before. For larger parties, printed invitations are best. Be sure to ask for a response. Your father or other relative should make the announcement by proposing a toast to you and your fiance.

After your engagement has been officially announced, send announcements to your hometown newspapers, college alumni newsletters, company newsletter, and other organizational publications where it is appropriate. Some newspapers require you to fill out a special form. Call the society/women's/lifestyle page editor and ask that one be sent to you. Ask also how far in advance they need the information and what their policy is on photographs. Some newspapers will not publish engagement photographs, but will publish a wedding picture. Some newspapers accept photographs of just the bride-to-be, others will accept a photograph of both of you. Larger newspapers charge for engagement and wedding announcements. Don't be shy about asking. The editor will usually assist you in preparing your announcement and paring it down to save you money.

If there is no special form, be sure your typed announcement (double-spaced) includes your names and those of both parents, the date and place of the wedding, and some background material, such as where you both went to school and where you are working now, where you plan to live, and perhaps some brief background information on your families, particularly if they are long-time residents of the area. Include your signature, name, address, home and business telephone numbers for verification purposes.

The Association of Bridal Consultants offers this example...

Mr. and Mrs. Craig Meyer, of St. Charles, Missouri, announce the engagement of their daughter, Miss Isabel Michelle Meyer, to Mr. Gary Harold Anforth, son of Mr. and Mrs. Michael Anforth of Fairfield, Connecticut. An October wedding is planned.Miss Meyer was graduated from Rumsey Hall School and is now a student at Sacred Heart University, Bridgeport, Connecticut. Mr. Anforth was graduated from Fairfield Prep and Yale University. He is employed by GTE Corp., Stamford, Connecticut.

If one or both of your parents are deceased, the Association suggests . . .

Mrs. (Mr.) Michael Bullard, of Chester, Vermont, announces the engagement of her (his) daughter, Miss Evelyn Louise Bullard, to Mr. Kenneth Howard Bailey, son of Mr. and Mrs. George Bailey, of Falls Church, Virginia. Miss Bullard also is the daughter of the late Michael Bullard. An October wedding is planned.

If your parents are divorced, here is a suggested format from the Association of Bridal Consultants . . .

Mrs. Vincent (Mrs. Wendy) Prucha, of Little Creek, Virginia, announces the engagement of her daughter, Miss Cynthia Lee Prucha, to Mr. Anthony Richard Dalton, son of Mr. and Mrs. John W. Dalton, of Washington, D.C. Miss Prucha also is the daughter of Mr. Vincent Prucha of Billings, Montana. An October wedding is planned.

If you are announcing your own engagement, the Association recommends this format . . .

Miss Faye Williams (daughter of the late Mr. and Mrs. Walter W. Williams—optional), of Princeton, California, announces her engagement to Mr. Philip B. Failla, son of Mr. and Mrs. Andrew L. Failla, of Westport, Washington. An October wedding is planned.

Give as much information as possible. If there isn't space for the entire announcement, the newspaper will edit it. Don't worry if you don't have a list of ancestors dating back to the Mayflower, your announcement is good news to those you know and also makes the newspaper more interesting in a time when all the news seems bad.

When you send a photograph, an 8" x 10" black-and-white glossy is preferable. Label it on the back with your name and address, and mail it with a cardboard backing to protect it. Mark the envelope, "Photograph - Do Not Bend." If you want the photograph back, include a stamped, self-addressed envelope.

If your engagement is going to be a long one, wait to alert the media until a month or two before the wedding. Now is a good time to set some of the other important dates before your calendar gets filled up—and it will! Schedule your bridesmaids' luncheon, which is usually one to two weeks before the wedding, the bachelors' party, three to four days before the wedding, and the rehearsal dinner.

The secret is out . . . and people may want to have parties in your honor. Schedule these important dates now, so you can tell your friends, when they ask, what dates are free for their parties.

Wedding Announcements

While we are on the subject of newspaper announcements, here is a sample of a wedding announcement from the Association of Bridal Consultants. As with the engagement announcement, it should be typewritten, double-spaced on standard typing paper. Be sure to include your name, address and telephone number.

Miss Susan Carla Wehn was married today to Mr. Timothy James Winkler. The marriage was performed at the Church of St. Francis of Assisi, Wakeeney, Kansas, by the Reverend Richard Wehn, the bride's brother.

The bride is the daughter of Mr. and Mrs. Arnold Wehn, of Lawrence, Kansas. Her grandparents are Mr. and Mrs. Bruce Wehn of Cleveland, Ohio, and Mr. and Mrs. Thomas P. Thomches, of Vernon, Connecticut.

Mr. Winkler is the son of Mr. and Mrs. Charles Winkler of Independence, Missouri. His grandparents are the late Mr. and Mrs. David Winkler of Independence, and Mrs. Janice Turek and the late Mr. Turek of Suffield, Massachusetts.

Mrs. Winkler wore satin trimmed with seed pearls and carried a bouquet of red roses and babies' breath, which was the floral theme of the wedding. Her veil, of tulle, is a family heirloom.

Miss Celia Wehn, the bride's sister, served as maid of honor. The bridesmaids were Miss Janis Winkler, the bridegroom's sister, and Miss Donna Johnson. Miss Lucy Wehn, a niece, served as flower girl, while Mr. Winkler's cousin, Thomas Winkler, was ring bearer.

Mr. Winkler's best man was Herbert Schoen of Upper Darby, Pennsylvania. The ushers were John Staples and Joseph Salome.

Mrs. Winkler graduated from Lawrence Community College and teaches in Wakeeney. Mr. Winkler is a civilian employee with the Army Reserve in Independence.

After a wedding trip, the couple will live in St. Charles, Missouri.

You can mention your job in the same way as Mr. Winkler's is in this example. If your parents are no longer alive, the wedding announcement should come from your nearest relative, godparent, close family friend or yourself.

Wedding Consultants: The Pros

If the zillions of details in planning your wedding are already overwhelming you, consider retaining a bridal consultant to organize it all and do much of the legwork that takes so much time. These experts can help you select flowers and work with the florist, plan the ceremony and reception, order the food and the cake and supervise the catering. They can even help you select a photographer and decide on the number of photographs you will require, research music and hire musicians if you want them, take you shopping for your bridal ensemble and attendants' dresses. In other words, they'll help you put it all together.

Ask your friends, especially those whose weddings you admired, and ask family members for recommendations and begin interviewing consultants. A list of "Colors for Brides" consultants is available, free of charge. Just return the coupon at the back of the book with a stamped, self-addressed envelope. These experts have been personally trained to understand how the seasonal color theory affects each aspect of your wedding—from your ring to the flower petals your guests may toss as you leave on your honeymoon. They can also guide you in choosing your tableware and linens and coordinating your home furnishing choices.

As Gerard J. Monaghan, President of the Association of Bridal Consultants in New Milford, Connecticut, says: "The use of bridal consultants is increasing because of the return to traditional, formal weddings that are more complicated and require more attention to etiquette. Brides and their mothers also have less time for planning because they are working."

Party planners, personal shoppers, your florist and caterer, also, can help you organize the myriad details. But if you decide to go ahead and plan everything yourself, be sure you check references and ask for examples of previous work—whether it's a taste of the cake or an album of photographs. Read their contracts carefully, making certain that terms of payment and dates of delivery are stated in full, and a guarantee of services honored. And, when you are shopping around for the best person for each service, ask ahead of time if they charge a consultation fee. Also, request references and call them.

Here is a checklist of what to ask for . . .

Photographer

Samples of previous work

Names of references

Exactly what is going to be in the package you are contracting for: number of photographs, size, album or sleeves

Can you keep the proofs? For how long?

Delivery date

What he will wear at your wedding? Make sure it complies with what the rest of the guests will wear.

Florist

Samples of previous work

References

Exactly what is going to be in the package you contract for: bouquets, ceremony decorations, altar flowers, boutonnieres, reception center pieces, etc.

Delivery time

Clean up?

Caterer

Samples of previous work

References

Exactly what is going to be in the package you contract: reception food (breakfast, brunch, lunch, tea, dinner, cocktail buffet)

Will he or she supply serving platters and flatware, glassware, tableware, tablecloths and napkins, a cake table, other tables and chairs, waiters, beverages, bartenders, clean-up crew?

What time will they arrive?

What will they wear?

Clean up begins when?

Baker

Taste samples of cakes available

Photos of previous work

References

Exactly what is going to be in the package you contract: cake, floral decorations, cake knife?

How much cake for the number of guests you expect?

Delivery time

Musicians

References

Range of music they can play

How many musicians

What equipment they will need

What you will be getting for your money: how many breaks, music selection, etc.

Arrival time

Departure time

Their dress?

Chapter 4
You on Your Wedding Day

Start with Your Gown

Whether it's an antique or high fashion, your bridal gown sets the mood for the entire day. Since most gowns must be ordered from the manufacturer, begin shopping for your special dress at least four months before the ceremony so that it will be perfect for you, in every way. Its style, color, and length dictate what everyone else must wear and how absolutely beautiful you look. Your dress is the most important purchase of all.

Of course, if you have inherited an antique dress from a beloved relative or ancestor, you may only have to have it altered to fit and to choose the appropriate accessories. Or if you have a piece of antique lace for a headdress, you have the beginnings of a lovely ensemble. You will be looking for accessories and gown to go with the romanticism of a bygone age.

If you must begin at the beginning in the search for the perfect gown, there are four things to consider: your color season, your clothing personality, the formality of the ceremony, and the place you'll be married. One way to start is to call a chosen bridal salon ahead of time and set up an appointment with the bridal consultant. Tell her how formal your ceremony will be, where and when it is taking place, and how much you have to spend. That way she can have a nice selection of dresses to show you when you arrive. Take a pair of shoes of a similar height to those you plan to wear, and the appropriate undergarments, so the fitting will be accurate.

More than 40 percent of all brides either make their own dress or have it made. Follow the same guidelines when designing your own dress or looking for the pattern that features the most flattering style for you. But whether you buy or make your dress, pay careful attention to details. Buttons, zippers, closings, and trims will all be handsewn in the more expensive dresses. Natural and imported fabrics are more costly than manmade ones. Look for fit and quality.

Setting the Mood with Your Personal Style

You know from your budget and the quiz you took in Chapter 1 the kind of wedding you want: ultraformal, formal, semiformal, or informal. Now let's consider what that says about you and your bridal costume.

If you have selected an ultraformal ceremony, you tend to be dramatic and to love huge parties, full of people. You like to be the center of attention and you want your wedding to be a splendid show, most likely in the evening when you really sparkle. Look for the most elaborate of full-length gowns (remember your budget, though!). For a winter wedding, your gown can be satin, peau de soie, faille, brocade, or velvet. In warmer months, forget the velvet, and look for organza, taffeta or lace. Your headdress should also be elaborate, in fur, feathers, exotic flowers, or sparkling jewels with a long veil and a cathedral or court train, silk or satin slippers, and a stole or cape for cold weather drives to and from the ceremony. As a dramatic personality you will delight in the extremes: satin, velvet, or brocade.

If you have chosen the formal ceremony, you are a more classic personality who likes things done with dignity in the time-honored traditional manner. You have probably opted for a late afternoon ceremony. Of all the personalities, you are most likely to inherit a lovely antique gown or at least a piece of antique lace. If not, you should search for a gown that has that timeless look, floor length, classic though sophisticated. Your veil can be long or short, with a simpler headdress of lace or pearls. Your train should be chapel or brush length. Court length is just too long and cumbersome for an afternoon wedding. As a classic you'll want a quiet matte or soft sheened fabric, a peau de soie, taffeta, faille, or silk crepe, or shantung.

The semiformal ceremony lends itself to romance, since it allows you the freedom to alter the traditions that seem too restrictive for your romantic soul. The semiformal ceremony may be held at any time or any place in which you feel beautiful. (One aside though. Before making any elaborate plans, check with your family clergy. Be sure your religious denomination permits a wedding at your chosen site.) But wherever you marry, surround yourself with flowers. Your dress can be floor-length or ankle-length in any of the beautiful, lustrous fabrics you crave, organza, taffeta and lace. But your veil and headdress should be much less elaborate. You may just want a simple wreath of flowers with an elbow length veil, or a picture hat, if you are wearing an antebellum dress.

Relaxed, friendly, and simple are the key words to the informal wedding preferred by down-to-earth natural personalities. Your dress can be simple and short or a raw silk or linen suit with a hat and no veil. Your ceremony can take place in a church, your home, or the office of a justice of the peace. Wherever it occurs, you'll want to be surrounded by your best friends and relatives and not be worried about rules and regulations.

What to Wear for Your Personal Style

Dramatic—Ultraformal

jeweled or fur headpiece or hat

severe, plain necklines from wedding band collars to plain jewel or low V necklines

long dress with straight or asymmetrical lines

long, tight sleeves, or exaggerated sleeves with fullness at top or bottom or sleeveless dress with long gloves

heavy, lustrous fabrics like satin, brocade or velvet fabrics

bold, ornate, or plain accessories and jewelry

Classic—Formal

pearl or lace headpiece decorated with pearls

bateau, sabrina, or portrait neckline

princess style or straight dress softened by gathers

long, traditional sleeves

matte fabrics with a soft sheen such as peau de soie, faille, taffeta or shantung

medium-sized accessories, simple jewelry

Romantic—Semiformal

floral wreath or headband or picture hat

low or off-the-shoulder neckline

puffed, bowed, or ruffled sleeves

full skirt with fitted waist

filmy, sheer fabrics such as organza, taffeta, and lace

dainty accessories and jewelry

Natural—Informal

simple or no headpiece or headband

necklines softened by a collar

tailored dress or suit with simple lines and gathered, gored, pleated or A-line skirt, tea length or shorter

textured matte fabrics such as linen, wool, or raw silk

simple jewelry and accessories, medium to large in size

The Right Place at the Right Time

Visit the place where you plan to marry before you set out to shop. Be sure to visit it at the same time of day.

Let's hope that your wedding location reflects the formality of your personality. Or you may have had no choice in the matter and have to make up for the incompatibility of the surroundings by decorating with your colors and flowers. Now take notice of the colors that are already in the room. Are they *warm* or *cool?* Most importantly, are they from *your* palette? If not, what can you do to offset them? In what season will the wedding take place? Is the room as formal as you wish your wedding to be? Is it ultramodern or traditional in feeling? Or does it need your personality to bring it to life? This room is your stage, be it church, synagogue, ballroom, living room, or the great outdoors. Your bridal dress is your costume in the play, and everything should go together.

Dramatic

This dramatic sheath, with its high neckline and long sleeves, sparkles with brilliant beading on Alencon lace. The satin train, bordered with lace, is detachable. The headpiece is a pouf attached to lace and beads. For the dramatic, ultraformal bride.

Photo: Courtesy of The House of Bianchi, reprinted courtesy of *Modern Bride*

Dramatic

This sophisticated sheath, in an all-over diamond pattern of Venice lace, with long, slender sleeves, is for the ultraformal, dramatic bride with maturity and style. The headpiece consists of branches of the same beads that trim the bodice.

Photo: Courtesy of The House of Bianchi, reprinted courtesy of *Modern Bride*

Photo: Courtesy of Bridal Originals

Classic

This classic dress of peau de soie has a Sabrina neckline, a beaded lace bodice, and long, traditional sleeves, with a softly gathered skirt ending in a chapel train—ideal for the classic bride having a formal wedding. Her veil is attached to a lace cap.

Classic
This graceful gown of matte finished taffeta and lace features long fitted sleeves and a softly gathered skirt with a traditional chapel length train. A classic dress for a formal or semiformal classic bride.

Photo: Courtesy of Christos

Romantic

For a formal wedding, this romantic bride wears an off-the-shoulder silk taffeta ballgown with a portrait neckline, puff sleeves with a cuff, a long torso and a chapel train, Calais lace appliqued on the sleeves, and a border of the chapel-length hem. The headpiece is of matching Calais lace.

Romantic

A fairy-tale dress with an embroidered, Alencon lace bodice, silk taffeta bow sleeves, and a curved low neckline, is for the truly romantic bride. The tulle skirt features a silk bow back with a removable train. The tiara, of Alencon lace with pearls, crystals, and sequins, has a long, shaped veil, touched with pearls.

You on Your Wedding Day

Natural

The natural bride will walk down the aisle in comfort and simplicity in this lace dress with a Sabrina neckline, dolman sleeves, and softly gathered skirt— perfect for an informal wedding.

Colors for Brides

Natural
With a swirl to her skirt and a beaming smile, the natural bride wears this simple lace, tea-length dress to her wedding and to many occasions afterwards.

Photo: Courtesy of Vogue/Butterick

You on Your Wedding Day

The Right White

The next consideration is color. There are as many shades of white as there are snowflakes. Winters need pure white to sparkle. If they are really dramatic, they can drift into the new icy pink. Summers need off whites. They can also be lovely in the new light, light colors—rose beige, petal pink, or soft blue. Springs, search for ivory or clear shell pink or peach. And, Autumns, you were made for oyster white or light warm beige or light, light gold.

Take this book with you when you shop, so you can check the fabrics against your palette. Of course, if you've had your colors done by a professional color consultant, take your fabric swatches. But whether you have color samples or not, when you are trying on dresses, be sure you are near natural light and can test the whites against your teeth, eyes, and skin. Look for the white that makes your skin look healthy and your eyes sparkle. Any white that makes you look pale or tired is certainly not for you on this magic day.

The Shape You Are In

The color of your dress should flatter your face, but the style should flatter your figure. If you are tall and slim, you can wear sophisticated high fashion with bold, sweeping lines. But if you are taller than 5'9", you may want to minimize your height somewhat with a dress that features a large collar or low neck, a tiered or flared skirt or one with horizontal trim all around it; raglan, dolman, or puff sleeves; and a Basque waistline or wide belt.

Shorter brides can look taller and slimmer in a dress that has vertical lines, appliques, or seams that run lengthwise. Look for an empire waist, a princess or A-line silhouette, small wedding band collar, sweetheart or deep-scalloped neckline; lace or beading at the neckline and shoulders, a narrow ribboned belt or none at all. Draw attention to your face with trims, and neckline and vertical lines. A number of manufacturers now specialize in petite sizes.

Too thin? Look for fullness in fabrics, sleeves and skirts. Textured fabrics, such as satins, velvets or linens, add curves and grace. To emphasize your tiny waist, add a distinctive sash in another color from your palette.

Too plump? Avoid very full skirts. Look for A-line or slim (but not tight!) skirts, narrow sleeves, and scooped or v-necks. All fullness should be in the front and sides, never in the back. Sometimes sleeves worn off the shoulder can be very attractive on those with beautiful, rounded shoulders.

Ask the bridal consultant to help you find the most flattering look. Maximize the positive, minimize the negative.

Good Training

Don't forget the back of your dress. You'll be standing with your back to the congregation for most of the ceremony, so this part of your dress needs special attention. Your veil and train will provide this back interest.

There are three main types of trains. The "brush" or "court" train is the shortest, just touching the floor. The "chapel" train falls about 1⅓ yards from your waist. And longest and most formal is the "cathedral" train which drops a full three yards from your waist. Needless to say, you should be tall enough to carry the cathedral train. It is for the ultraformal ceremony only, held in a very large church or synagogue.

Your train can be formed from the back panels of your wedding gown or be attached with hooks and eyes at your shoulders, yoke or waist. If it is detachable, it can be removed for the reception to make dancing easier. For a semiformal or informal wedding, no train is necessary.

Topping It All Off

The veil is an ancient tradition, and a head covering is still required for all religious ceremonies. The second-time bride, however, should not wear a face or blush veil. A hat or headdress is more appropriate. A veil can be a lace mantilla or triple-tiered silk illusion. In keeping with your train, your veil can be a four-yard cathedral length, a three-yard chapel length, elbow-length bouffant or a three-tiered fingertip style. The more formal your dress, the longer your veil should be.

Your bridal hat should complement your dress and your hairstyle. Choose from wreaths, half-hats, turbans, face-framers, caps, toques, pillboxes, derbies, and picture hats. A wreath of fresh flowers is a lovely touch for semiformal and informal weddings; a jeweled tiara, or cap for ultraformal and formal weddings. Picture hats, pillboxes, and derbies go with less formal attire; Juliet caps, glittering headbands, and half-hats elaborately designed and trimmed with lace, beads, jewels, flowers, fur, or feathers for formal styles.

You on Your Wedding Day

When you are selecting this "crowning glory," style your hair the way you plan to wear it on your wedding day. Try on the various styles of headpieces with your dress, so that you can see whether or not it goes with your dress and flatters your face. Short-sleeved dresses need simple headdresses. Picture hats go with open necklines and long hair. Juliet caps set off curly hair, long or short. A mantilla goes with almost any dress style or hair length. Work with your hairdresser and bridal consultant.

If you want to try something new, visit your hairdresser with your headpiece about six to eight weeks before the wedding. A new cut or a permanent should be done four weeks ahead. Schedule an appointment with your hairdresser a week before the wedding to trim the ends and touch up any roots that may be showing by then.

As a dramatic Winter personality, you will look best with your hair in a smooth, sleek style, whether worn up or down. Keep it off your face to emphasize your chiseled bone structure. Your makeup should emphasize your eyes and lips, with high contrasts. Put your blue red, wine, or plum, rose or pink lips, cheeks and nails, black or brown-black mascara, and gray-lilac eyelids on a cool rose ivory or rose beige foundation.

If you're a classic Summer, you should style your hair in a soft pageboy, French twist or roll. Your makeup should emphasize your eyes, cheeks, and lips in balanced, cool light-to-medium colors: pink ivory or pink beige foundation; pink, rose, mauve, or light plum lipstick, blush, and nails; charcoal gray mascara and mauve shadow.

Romantic Spring, you should wear long, loose curls piled high and tempered with tendrils. Your makeup should play on your eyes, cheeks and lips in warm light-to-medium colors: peach ivory or peach beige foundation, warm pink, peach-pink, coral pink, light true red lipstick, nails and blush, with brown mascara and ivory, warm brown and peach shadow.

Natural Autumn? You should wear your hair in the casual, windblown hairstyles you love, with makeup that emphasizes your eyes and leaves lips and cheeks to nature: warm beige ivory or peach beige or golden beige foundation; with brick, terra cotta, cinnamon, apricot, or peach lipstick, nails and blush and brown mascara over champagne, warm brown and gold shadow.

There's going to be a lot of kissing and crying on this special day, so make sure your mascara is waterproof. Your lipcolor will also last longer if you powder your lips lightly, outline them with a pencil and fill in with color. If you're good with makeup, do it yourself. If not, consider having a makeup artist do it for you . . . or have a makeup lesson a week or two before and practice, practice, practice until you have mastered the look. Be sure to check your makeup colors in different types of lighting, natural and artificial, depending on where your ceremony will take place and your reception will be.

Keep your makeup and hair simple, no matter how flamboyant your personality. This is the day to let your dress and flowers say it all, as your natural beauty shines through, quietly enhanced by your makeup. Now may be the time to spice up your hair color, however. Ask your hairdresser to help you be a little more Winter, Summer, Spring, or Autumn.

UncommonScents

On your wedding day you want to wear a subtle, a very subtle, perfume that reflects your season almost as much as your palette. Winters go for the Fareastern and exotic floral scents of Shalimar, Chantilly, Tabu, Bal a Versailles, Emeraude, Magic Noire, Vanderbilt, Oscar de la Renta, Dioressence, Giorgio, Gianfranca Ferre, Adolfo, Bill Blass, Chloe, Charles of the Ritz, Halston Night, Estee, Youth Dew, or Opium.

Summers, search out the single flower or soft floral bouquet of Chanel No. 5, Arpege, Sortilege, Madame Rochas, White Linen, L'Air du Temps, Joy, or White Shoulders.

Springs, you want that light, fresh, sweet floral or fruity scent of Fidgi, Norell, Charlie, Lauren, Lou Lou, Anais Anais, Diorella, or Diorissimo.

You woodsy Autumns, search for the spicy, fruity scents of Halston, Cabochard, Miss Dior, Ma Griffe, and Coriandre.

To the Tips of Your Toes

Slip your feet into shoes that are pretty but comfortable. You'll be on your feet for a long time. You'll need slippers of silk or satin in a classic pump, dyed to match the white of your dress. For the more elaborate dresses, shoes can be trimmed in lace, beads, or jewels to match. Open-toed or open-heeled shoes are not appropriate, except for the most informal wedding. Be sure that you and your bridesmaids all have the same height heels on your shoes.

And don't forget your hosiery. Winters and Summers, look for cool tones, white or off-white or delicate blush, sheer or with lace. Springs and

Autumns can wear the sheerest ivory, champagne, or warm nude shades. Your hosiery should always blend with your dress and shoes.

Hanes Hosiery reports that the traditional garter dates back to the Middle Ages and the beginnings of England's oldest and most important knighthood, the Order of the Garter. According to the legend, the Countess of Salisbury dropped her garter while dancing and Edward III returned it to her, discreetly commenting, "May he be ashamed who thinks ill of it." Later this custom was taken over by a rowdy troop of wedding guests who followed the wedding couple right into their bridal suite, stealing the bride's garter and stockings and tossing the garter over their heads. This went on until the garter landed on the bride or groom's nose. The guest who tossed it would be the next to be married. Hanes suggests that the modern bride who wishes to escape the traditional garter toss should try their thigh-high stockings with eyelet ruffles.

Gloves and Other Accessories

Gloves are a traditional part of your bridal costume, but are not really necessary for the semiformal or informal wedding. In the ultraformal and formal ceremony, long white kid gloves should be worn with short-sleeved dresses. If you are the dramatic type, you may want gloves accented with lace, jewels, or other embellishments to complement your gown. The third finger on your left-hand glove should be gently slit so that your groom can slip your ring on. After the service this glove finger can be repaired, so you can wear the gloves again.

Besides your bouquet, you may want to carry your own or a beloved relative's prayer book or handkerchief. Bridal handbags are also available in all sorts of styles to complement your dress, from white satin to delicate lace, with jeweled clasps and gold-plated frames, to antique frames and clasps.

Jewelry should be kept at a minimum for all but the ultraformal type. Ultraformals, if you have room on your body for something else, make it an elegant necklace or showy pair of earrings. Make sure they are in keeping with the rest of your ensemble. For everyone else, a pair of simple earrings and a bracelet or necklace that goes with the neck of your dress are all you really need. You'll soon have a new ring to add to your finery.

Fittings

The store where you purchase your dress will require at least one fitting once your dress arrives. This is why it is important to order your dress three to six months in advance. You must allow plenty of time for further adjustments after you try it on for the first time. You should schedule the photographer to take your wedding portrait at the final fitting to avoid at least one project on the big day itself.

Dressing the Other Characters

We'll go into much more detail about your attendants' dresses in the next chapter. But don't forget them as you plan your bridal costume. Your attendants and your mother and your future mother-in-law should all dress in the style you choose. If your dress is ultraformal, so must theirs be. If your dress is cool white, theirs should be in the Winter or Summer palettes. If your dress is a warm white, theirs should be in the Spring or Autumn palettes. If you choose something very sophisticated, they will too. *You* are the star, but don't forget your co-stars as you make your plans.

A Glossary of Styles and Fabrics

Here's what all those terms you'll hear when you enter the bridal salon mean. . .

Bodices

Basque   A closely-fitted bodice, joined by seaming from shoulder to waist.

Bodice   The top of a dress.

Bolero   A short open jacket with long or short sleeves.

Cummerbund   A wide sash, closely fitted to the midriff.

Fitted bodice   Designed to hug the body.

Strapless   Reveals the shoulders and is usually worn with a bolero or jacket during the wedding ceremony.

Silhouettes

Ballgown   Low or off-the-shoulder neckline and a very full skirt.

Princess   Closely fitted top with gradually flaring skirt cut in continuous pieces.

Redingote   Fitted coatdress with flared skirt worn over matching or coordinating dress.

Sheath   Straight, narrow dress usually with a detachable train.

Decorations

Applique   Cut-out design applied to the surface of fabric which may contrast in color or texture or both.

Beading   Openwork through which beads are applied or ribbon is run.

Embroidery   Ornamental needlework done either by hand or machine.

Ruching   Pleated or gathered frill used as trim.

Collars and Necklines

Asymmetrical   Neckline that falls diagonally to one side.

Batteau   A boat-shaped neckline, usually trimmed with lace.

Bertha collar   A wide, flat collar, 9" to 18" long, attached to the yoke of the blouse.

Cowl neckline   A soft neckline, draped around the neck in horizontal folds.

Decolletage   A lowcut, usually rounded, neckline.

Fichu   A draped, capelike collar usually of sheer or lacelike fabric.

Jewel   Outlines the natural neckline.

Mandarin   Narrow, standing collar that does not meet in the center in front.

Queen Anne   Higher on sides and back and open to bra line in front, ending in a sweetheart shape.

Queen Elizabeth   High portrait collar that stands up in the back ending with a "v" in front.

Sabrina   Straight neckline usually trimmed with lace that begins about two inches inside the shoulder line.

Sweetheart   Heart-shaped neckline that begins about two inches inside the shoulder line.

Wedding band   High Victorian neckline usually of lace encircling the base of the neck.

Fabrics

Batiste   A sheer, fine cotton, named after Jean Baptiste, a French weaver.

Brocade   A formal fabric with an all-over woven design of raised flowers or figures, enhanced by contrasting surfaces, colors or metallic threads on a satin ground.

Charmeuse   A soft, shiny fabric that is made from silk or silklike fibers that drapes beautifully and is used for very high-style dramatic dresses.

Chiffon   Very light, transparent fabric in plain weave silk or silklike fibers, good for soft, feminine dresses.

Crepe   Fabric woven from tightly twisted yarns of silk, wool, rayon or synthetics so that the finished fabric has a rippled or crinkled surface.

Crepe de chine   Fabric with a soft look made of silk or silklike fibers and used for less formal dresses.

Eyelet   A decorative fabric in which holes are systematically cut out and the open areas surrounded with embroidery, often in floral patterns.

Faille   Slightly shiny silk or silklike fabric with a rib weave, sometimes stiff, sometimes soft and pliable, depending on the weight of the fabric.

Grosgrain   Fabric with a pronounced crosswise rib, often used for ribbons.

Illusion   Sheer, fine tulle used for veils.

Lace   Fabric woven of cotton, rayon, nylon, or silk in different motifs, named after the towns in which they originated: Venetian lace is from Italy; Alencon, Calais, Chantilly, and Lyon from France; Brussels from Belgium.

Moire   Silk or silklike fabric with a watermark finish.

Organdy   Light, transparent, but stiff cotton fabric with eyelet trim, used for overskirts or pinafores.

Organza   A crisp but sheer fabric made of silk or silklike fibers and often appliqued, good for romantic styles.

Pique   corded cotton fabric, used for summer weddings.

Peau de soie   Soft, but firm silk or silklike fabric with dull satinlike surface, used for classic, formal dresses.

Point d'Esprit   Net fabric woven in a dot pattern.

Shantung   Silk or silklike fabric of slub yarns giving an irregular textured appearance.

Satin   Silk or silklike fabric with a matte back and lustrous surface.

Taffeta   A fine plain weave fabric of silk or silk blends with a slight sheen. May be solid or printed or woven in two colors to produce an irridescent effect.

Tulle   A fine, very lightweight, machinemade net used for bridal veils and for overdraping on bridal dresses.

Velvet   Fabric with a soft, thick pile woven of silk, rayon or nylon.

Velveteen   Made of cotton with less sheen and more body than other types of velvet.

Voile   Fine, semitransparent fabric of plain-weave cotton, good for country weddings.

Headpieces

Branches   Decorative beads extending from headpiece.

Derby   A hat with a dome-shaped crown and narrow brim, which is fitted with a veil or covered with fabric for wedding wear.

Headband   A plain or very decorative band worn on the head with or without a veil.

Juliet cap   A round cap that fits the head, often decorated with seed pearls.

Mantilla   A lace scarf that covers head and shoulders.

Picture   A hat with a large floppy brim usually trimmed with flowers and ribbons.

Pillbox   A small, round hat with a flat crown and straight sides.

Tiara   Jeweled headpiece shaped like a crown.

Toque   A small, brimless hat, usually worn to one side.

Wreath   A circle of flowers and other decorations to which the veil has been attached that fits at the back of the head.

Hemlengths

Ankle length   A skirt that reveals the ankles.

Floor length   Hem falls about one-half to one inch from the floor.

Handkerchief   Sculpted, tea length hemline.

Tea length   Falls several inches above the ankles.

Waltz length   Same as tea length.

Skirts

A-line   A skirt that is flat in front, gradually widening to a full hem.

Apron   Overskirt which joins at the waist in the back but not at the hem.

Ballet skirt   A full skirt that falls gracefully to the ankle.

Bouffant   A full, voluminous skirt.

Bubble   Fabric is attached to the lining at the hemline to create a bubble effect.

Bustle   Gathering of fabric at the back of the dress just below the waistline.

Butterfly   A bow or other embellishment at back of the dress just below the waistline.

Circular   Falling from the waist to form a complete circle at the hem.

Dirndl   A full, gathered skirt.

Full   Full, but not as voluminous, as the bouffant.

Panniers   Gathered fabric over the hips.

Peplum   Ruffle or short, flared extension from waistline of skirt.

Pouf   Overskirt caught up with a flower, bow, or ribbon.

Tiered   Falls in a series of layers of graduated length.

Trumpet   Flares at or below the knees, also called mermaid skirt.

Sleeves

Bishop   Gathered and full to the cuffs, which may be elongated.

Bow   Short sleeve made of looped fabric, worn on or off the shoulder.

Cap   A short, fitted sleeve that barely covers the top of the arm.

Cape   A graceful short loose sleeve that forms a "cape" from the shoulder.

Cuff   A small puffed sleeve with a band around the bottom.

Dolman   A large set-in sleeve with deep armsets.

Draped   Fabric draped in bias folds to form a sleeve.

Fitted   A long traditional sleeve with very little, if any, fullness.

Gauntlet   An arm-covering of lace or other fabric used instead of gloves.

Gibson   Full at the shoulder and fitted at the wrist but more controlled than the leg-o-mutton.

Juliet   A very full short puff at the shoulder, then long and tight to the wrist.

Leg o' mutton   Sleeve with very full puff at the shoulder and a fitted forearm.

Poet   Pleated at the shoulder with fullness to the cuff.

Point   Long sleeve that ends below the wrist in a point.

Puff   Very full, short sleeve, gathered at the shoulder.

Raglan   Sleeve with long armhole line extending to the neckline.

Trains

Brush train   A train that just brushes the floor.

Cathedral   Extends a full three yards from the waist.

Chapel   Extends a full one-and-half yards from the waist.

Court   Slightly shorter than the chapel train.

Sweep   Slightly longer than a brush train.

Watteau   Train attached at the back yoke shoulder of the gown.

Veils

Ballet, tea, or waltz length   One or more layers of ankle length veiling.

Blusher   One layer of veiling worn over the face before the ceremony and lifted up and back over the head by the groom during the ceremony, ordinarily attached to a long veil in back.

Cathedral   Three-and-one-half yards falling from headpiece and extending over a cathedral train.

Elbow   Extending to the elbow.

Fingertip   One or more layers of veiling extending to the fingertips.

Flyaway   Multiple layers of veiling that brush the shoulders and are usually worn with an informal ankle-length dress.

Pouf   Gathering of veiling attached to the back of headpiece.

Waistlines

Dropped   Extending several inches below the natural waistline.

Empire   High-waisted, straight silhouette, derived from styles of the French Empire and Empress Josephine.

Natural   Bodice and skirt are joined at the natural waist.

Raised   Approximately one inch above the natural waistline.

Chapter 5
The Bridegroom and Members of the Wedding

Everyone Wants to Be Part of the Fun

Everyone who loves you will want to be part of your wedding. Your mother and father, your fiance's mother and father, your brothers and sisters, his brothers and sisters, your best friends, his best friends. . . . How can you include all of them in the ceremony? Unless you are having a huge ultraformal wedding, you can't. But there is a special role for everyone.

Your Groom's Attendants

You and your fiance should decide how many attendants you'll need and who they should be. There should be one usher or groomsman for each fifty guests. Besides his ushers, your groom must decide who will be his best man. The best man does not help seat guests, but stands with the groom to await your arrival at the altar. The best man has many duties. He supervises the ushers' fittings, can be the host at a bachelor party for the groom, helps him organize the tickets and papers for the honeymoon and to dress before the wedding, drives him to the ceremony, gives the clergy the groom's fee, and acts as one of the two witnesses who sign the marriage certificate. At the reception, the best man offers the first toast, makes sure the bride's and groom's luggage is taken to their car and that it is ready for their getaway. He may also take the groom's wedding outfit back to the rental shop.

The usher's main responsibility is to greet and seat guests at the ceremony, the bride's on the left and the groom's on the right. (At an orthodox Jewish ceremony, this is reversed.) The head usher should be chosen not only for the friendship he has provided the groom over the years but also because of the experience he has had as an usher at other weddings. He should be able to quietly supervise the other ushers while the best man is busy helping the groom.

The ushers make a very important contribution to the smoothness of the entire ceremony. Select them with care.

The Bridesmaids

There is no set rule about how many bridesmaids you can have. The traditional number is four; but you may select twelve if you want. And, if you are having a small informal wedding, just a maid or matron of honor may be all you need to hold your bouquet and the groom's ring if you are having a double ring ceremony, and help you with the myriad details of the wedding ahead of time. Some brides now have both a matron and a maid of honor. If you do, the maid of honor should perform these duties for you. She is also responsible for running errands, giving you a bridal shower, helping select a gift for you from all your bridesmaids, helping you dress before the wedding, and standing next to the groom in the receiving line at the reception. If you are having an ultraformal wedding and a cathedral train, the maid of honor will also be your train bearer, unless you designate a young boy for this job.

Junior Members of the Wedding

Junior bridesmaids can be a charming addition to your wedding party. They are generally young girls between ten and fifteen who will be thrilled to be part of your great day. They should be dressed in smaller versions of the bridesmaids' costumes or in similar dresses more appropriate to their age. They should be invited to the showers with your other attendants. You may also want to ask the young daughter of a friend or relative to be your flower girl. A flower girl is usually under six years old. She will strew your path with paper or silk rose petals as she walks down the aisle.

The job of ring bearer is also optional but a sweet young boy carrying your rings on an antique pillow is a sight to capture the heart of many a wedding guest. He should also be under six years old, but be responsible and self-confident enough to carry out his duties. The little ring bearer at a recent wedding I attended didn't make it all the way down the aisle. Sam was only four, and stopped in confusion when he saw where his mother was sitting. The wedding party marched on. The rings are carried on a white velvet or satin cushion, secured by thread or pins. The best man takes the rings from the ring bearer, but everyone might feel more secure if the best man is in charge of the real rings while the ring bearer carries fake ones. A young train bearer, dressed in white, can be assigned to walk behind the bride, holding her train. The Association of Bridal Consultants warns, "Unless they are well rehearsed—and very well behaved—it often is safer to leave the train unattended."

An ultraformal wedding can also include junior ushers. These boys, usually young relatives of the bridegroom, walk in the procession and recession dressed just like the ushers. They are generally ten to fourteen years old. If there are two of them, they can be in charge of placing the pew ribbons.

For simplicity's sake, I'd like to tell you to choose attendants who share your color season. And if you ask close relatives to attend you, very likely they will be of similar coloring. But I know that it is frequently impossible and it should not be a limiting factor. Try to include people among your attendants who represent families and those important friends you want to share in all the fun of your wedding. It is better to have too many members of the wedding, than to hurt someone's feelings. But remember, if everyone can't be an attendant, there are many other jobs, like reading a lesson during the service, giving a party or shower, running errands. There are duties for everyone who cares about you. *Delegate, delegate, delegate.* People want to help you.

When you've decided who will be your attendants, call them to extend a personal invitation and follow up with a little note. One bride sent each of her bridesmaids a small nosegay with her letter. It was a special way of saying how pleased she was they would be her attendants.

The Mothers

This is a precious time for you and your mother. It is a time to plan together for an event she has dreamed about for you since the day you were born. It should be a happy time. Of course, there will be tension. After all, you are both adults now and may have different ideas about how you want things done. But try to keep the joy of the occasion in mind whenever things seem stressful. Somehow everything comes together on the big day.

You and your mother will be orchestrating all the arrangements for the wedding and reception; but even after the wedding itself your mother will be busy. She may still have out-of-town guests to entertain. Following an afternoon wedding, for instance, she and your father may host a supper for these well-traveled guests and relatives, or a brunch the next day. She will mail the announcements the day after the wedding, and answer telegrams sent to you while you are away. She should send handwritten notes to those whose late gifts arrive while you are on your honeymoon. She will wrap and freeze the groom's cake or the leftover top layer of your bridal cake, so that it can be brought out to celebrate your first anniversary. She is also responsible for taking your bridal gown to the cleaner to be cleaned and packed so that it will not rot or stain. After all this, she'll be ready to take a second honeymoon herself!

Your mother may purchase her dress first, but she and your groom's mother should consult beforehand about styles, colors, and lengths to complement each other and your palette. Both should look for colors in their own palettes that blend with colors you have selected for the rest of the wedding party. For instance, if you are a Summer and your mother is a Winter, and you have picked lilac for your attendants, she may want to select icy violet in her Winter palette. And your Autumn mother-in-law may want to choose a dress in periwinkle from her palette. Then everyone will blend. Your mother may want to wear a small hat or headband with a veil, or even a flower in her hair if she is particularly young and charming. A fur can be thrown over her shoulders if the weather is cool, and she should carry a small purse. Both mothers will have corsages, of course. Some may prefer to wear theirs on their wrist or pinned to their purse.

Don't forget to include your fiance's mother in your planning. She can feel left out, since she has no real responsibility for the wedding. Traditionally, the parents of the groom give the rehearsal dinner, including close relatives, friends, and the wedding party. You and your mother need not be concerned

The Groom and Members of the Wedding

about the planning duties for this delightful last evening before your married life begins except to share your color choices. Your future mother-in-law must also prepare her family's guest list. She may also want to give you a luncheon or give a party for both of you to meet your fiance's family friends. Call her frequently to discuss the wedding, as your plans proceed. You'll be setting the tone for your future relationship and be glad you did it so well.

The Fathers

Your father and your fiance's father also need your attention, your father in particular. He will be leading you down the aisle and symbolically giving you away to your new life. It is a happy time and a sad one for him because it marks the end of an era when he was the man you loved most.

Your future father-in-law will help his wife plan the rehearsal dinner and host that lovely evening event. Your fiance should consult with him about the honeymoon. He will probably enjoy helping him to plan it, and will most likely be full of reminiscences about his own honeymoon that make this a happy time for father and son.

Dressing the Members of Your Wedding

The Men. Each person pays for his or her own wedding outfit, although the groom provides ties, gloves, and boutonnieres for his attendants. Let's start with the men because their outfits have the least flexibility. Although today the rules are less rigid, it's good to know what they are. And your man must look his very best for this day of days.

Unless he owns evening clothes or formal wear, the groom and his groomsmen will have to rent their wedding outfits through a formalwear specialist, department store, or tailor. Six to eight weeks before the wedding, the groom should arrange for fittings for both fathers, himself, and his groomsmen. Have him make certain that the clothes are of very high quality and well-tailored. You don't want him looking less elegant than you do. Each man should count on spending $50 to $70 to rent his outfit.

The store will provide a "mail measurement card" for those who live out of town. Their local formalwear specialist can measure them, then they will return the card to the groom, who will take it to his tailor and arrange for the outfits to be ready for a final fitting when his attendants arrive—at least one day ahead of time, please. Except for hose and underwear, the formalwear store will provide everything from jacket to suspenders, studs, and cufflinks. For the ultraformal or formal wedding, white pearl cuff links and studs; precious or semiprecious stones, black or gray pearl, or plain gold must be worn. Any discreet jewelry is appropriate for the semiformal or informal wedding. Dress shirts have pleated fronts and a set of buttonholes for the studs.

Shoes are usually available for rental as well. Dress shoes must be worn for ultraformal and formal weddings. There are black, lightweight, plain patent leather opera pumps, oxfords or dress boots; calf oxfords or slip-ons; pumps in silk, calf, or velvet. Hose must be black silk or lisle.

Again, the groom provides his attendants with gloves, ties, and boutonnieres. White gloves should be worn for ultraformal and formal evening weddings, formal or semiformal daytime call for gray gloves.

For the ultraformal evening wedding, the groom and his attendants should wear a black or midnight blue coat with satin lapels and tails, matching trousers, white-pique vest, white linen or silk dress shirt with wing-collar and pleated front, and a white bow tie. A cummerbund may be substituted for the vest. A truly dramatic groom can don a top hat and white gloves.

For the ultraformal daytime wedding the men should wear an oxford gray or black cutaway coat with striped trousers, gray vest, striped ascot, and white shirt with winged collar. A black or gray contoured long or short jacket is also appropriate.

The men at a formal evening wedding should wear black tuxedos or dinner jackets with black striped pants, white wing-collared shirts, a black vest, or cummerbund and black bow tie. During the day they wear gray or black morning jackets, striped trousers, gray vests, white soft-collared shirts, and gray-and-white striped ties. Homburgs and gloves are nifty accessories.

The semiformal and informal weddings allow the men as much freedom as you have, although a black, dark gray, or navy business suit always looks good. In the summer, navy blazers with white flannel trousers look smart, as do white or natural jackets and dark worsted trousers. Dark or white shoes may be worn in warmer climates. Shirts should be your wedding color palette, if possible.

The ring bearer wears a dark Eaton suit with dark knee-high socks and black shoes or a white suit with white socks and shoes in summer or tropical temperatures.

Colors for Brides

Photo: Courtesy Raffinati from The Robert Wagner Collection

Ultraformal Evening Wedding
White Tie and White Tails for hot weather. White Tie and Black
Tails for all seasons.

The Groom and Members of the Wedding

Formal Evening Wedding
The Tuxedo

Colors for Brides

Ultraformal or Formal Daytime Wedding
The Cutaway

The Groom and Members of the Wedding

Formal or Semiformal Daytime Wedding
The Stroller

Colors for Brides

Here is a tip from a well-known New York hairdresser: have the groom and his attendants get their hair cut four or five days before the wedding so it doesn't look freshly "shorn."

The Bridesmaids. The bridesmaids are your attendants and their dresses must reflect the colors, style, and formality you have chosen for your wedding. You and your attendants should "go together." For this reason, many brides choose dresses in exactly the same style as their own, with the same sleeves, neckline, waist, and back details, for instance. It is easy to do this if you are having all the dresses made by a seamstress. Vogue-Butterick, McCalls, and Simplicity have many patterns to help. And, many dress designers and manufacturers produce bridal dresses with bridesmaid costumes to match.

Since the bridesmaids can wear the lovely colors you have chosen from your palette other than white, their outfits reflect the theme of the wedding even more than yours does. For an ultraformal wedding, they may wear the silver and glitter. For the garden wedding, bright-colored flowers and straw hats and ballet shoes will set the mood.

But keep the same guidelines of color, clothing personality. and budget in mind when you select dresses for your attendants as you did when selecting your own. If you have asked a soft, feminine friend to attend you, don't dress her in severe aubergine that makes her look like an overstuffed eggplant. Consider all your bridesmaids when you make a selection. Let their dresses emphasize their positive features, and soften the less than perfect. Follow the guidelines given in Chapter 4 for your wedding dress.

Because the bridesmaids usually pay for their own dresses, do try to select a style that can be worn for more than just the wedding. But how many of us have a closet full of never-worn-again bridesmaid's dresses? If you and your bridesmaids are on a budget, be reasonable, and choose something everyone can afford to wear for one fun-filled event and not feel too bad if they never wear it again. Some designers are coming out with dresses with removable sleeves or redingotes to make them useable after the wedding. And, if you are very inventive, you may be able to find costumes outside the bridal department that can be worn for the day and many times afterwards. Especially for an ultraformal evening wedding, you may succeed in finding evening dresses that complement yours and which your bridesmaids can dance in through many other evenings. Strapless gowns can be made into bridesmaid dresses by adding a bolero, capelet, or jacket.

For the ultraformal or formal wedding, your maids should wear long dresses, short veils or headpieces, and gloves to complement the sleeves of the dress. For the semiformal wedding, the dresses can be short, but dressy. For the informal wedding, the maids can wear short dresses or suits.

Winter brides with your icy white dress, look for sparkling jewel tones for your bridesmaids. Or if yours will be an ultraformal wedding, try the new black-and-white color schemes. This dramatic color combination is only for the most sophisticated city wedding, however, and all the bridesmaids should be self-confident Winters who can carry it off. Many designers are coming out with rich, dark, bridesmaids' costumes, very different from the traditional pastels. And these colors can be very successful, especially for a winter or autumn wedding.

Summer, with your delicate antique white dress or soft tint of pink or blue, dress your bridesmaids in those dusty roses, mauves, lavenders, blues, and periwinkles. You are a softer version of a Winter so you are probably tending toward the quieter, more traditional formal wedding. These elegant, refined colors will complement the more muted tone of your wedding.

Autumn, in your oyster white or ivory gown, surround yourself with attendants in mid-toned turquoise, periwinkle, gold, moss green, or even coffee. Be careful with your greens, however, because they can make a Winter or a Summer maid look pretty muddy. Periwinkle or mid-toned turquoise is a wiser choice if your attendants are not all autumn leaves.

Light, bright Spring bride, dress your maids in clear shell pink, peach, aqua, or periwinkle, or even dove gray. The mood will be as sunny as you are, delicate and feminine.

Now you know why I've recommended marrying in your own season. The colors of your palette will seem most natural during the time of year where they are ever-present: a red and white Christmas wedding for a Winter; a Summer or Spring outdoor garden wedding surrounded by the flowers that make these seasons so appealing; an Autumn wedding in a harvest mood.

But if you are a very versatile personality and your best friends' style and coloring is just as diverse, choose those universally attractive colors of periwinkle, coral, or turquoise for your bridesmaids and their bouquets. Everyone looks good in these three colors, but make sure their makeup complements the look. Lipsticks, nail polish, blush, and eye makeup should be the same for all the bridesmaids. They are a bridal chorus and should look it.

Headpieces for your bridesmaids are another important part of their costume. They should be similar to your headpiece, but simpler. Real flowers, short veils, turbans, caps, combs, wreaths, headbands, hairbows, or barrettes can be flattering for almost any length hair or face shape. They should be decorated to coordinate with your flowered, feathered, furred, or jeweled headpiece. Large headbands can top any hair style and unify the look of your bridesmaids, despite great differences in hair coloring and length. Decorate them with the flowers of the bridesmaids' bouquets, or sparkling jewels for a dramatic glitter, feathers, even silk autumn leaves. Or, try having the bridesmaids comb their hair back under a large romantic hairbow in the colors of your wedding palette. You might want to provide a single flower for their hair during the reception if the headpiece for the wedding is going to be elaborate or cumbersome. With the single flower they'll look lovely, but have more freedom.

Watch those earrings and other jewelry! Earrings are always a most appreciated gift and you could make your bridesmaids' gifts be the earrings you want them to wear for the wedding.

For ultraformal and formal weddings, gloves should be white or in a color that matches the dresses. The length of the dresses' sleeves determines the length of the gloves.

Remember, hosiery is another accessory you mustn't overlook. There are so many colors to choose from. Hanes Hosiery recommends a subtle evening shade that will take the bride and her attendants from wedding to reception with a glow. It is available in pantyhose and a thigh high lace top stocking.The palest peach, light golden-brown and soft amber for Springs and Autumns; a soft blue-green, light gray, sheer lilac, silver, jet black, pearl, and pink for Winter and Summer palette weddings.

Pumps, flats, or ballet shoes can be dyed to match or harmonize with their dresses. Dressy white sandals for an informal summer wedding, or daring silver for a dramatic ultraformal or formal winter wedding could grace the feet of your attendants as they trip down the aisle with you.

If your bridesmaids are scattered all over the country, it's up to you to order their dresses. The store can supply you with measurement forms (similar to those your bridegroom gets for his attendants) or a list of dimensions the dressmaker or store will need for each maid. Send one to each bridesmaid with a return envelope, along with tips on how to take the measurements. Most likely each will be asked to fill in her bust, waist, hips, height, weight, and dress size and return it to you. Collect the cards and order the dresses yourself. Get everyone's shoe and glove size and order these, too. Have the shoes dyed at the same time in the same place. Choose adjustable headpieces, such as headbands or hats with elastic inserts. Try to get your bridesmaids to arrive at least a couple days before the wedding, so that alterations can be made if necessary.

The Flower Girl. Your dear little flower girl should wear a tea-length or short dress in a color that blends with the other attendants' dresses. She will carry a basket provided by the florist filled with rose petals to drop delicately along the aisle as she precedes you. A floral wreath, colored ribbon, headband, or barrette in a simpler version than yours should top her head, with white gloves or mitts on her hands.

Gifts for Your Attendants

You will want to select something special for your bridesmaids, a gift that will remind each of her part in your wedding. Jewelry, including the earrings for their wedding outfits, a bracelet or necklace are always appropriate. A special book you have particularly enjoyed inscribed by you, silver picture frames, hand-painted scarves, embroidered handkerchiefs, perfume—you know what each of your good friends will appreciate. Make each gift a special tribute, especially to your maid of honor who will be working very hard to help you.

Your fiance should also shop carefully for the gifts for his ushers. Cuff links, pen and pencil sets, money clips, books, objets d'art—whatever he chooses, they should all be alike. And, he should spend a little extra time and money on his best man. A watch, a fine leather billfold, a piece of sporting equipment, these are all appropriate for this very important person in your wedding.

If a friend or relative performs a special job at the wedding for which he or she may not be compensated but for which you are especially grateful, you'll want to offer a gift of thanks. Whether this person plays an instrument or sings at your wedding or reception, or performs some other vital service like addressing all the invitations in her beautiful calligraphy, choose the gift with care.

What you select for each other is a very personal matter. Often the bridegroom presents his bride with pearls, a pendant, or locket she will wear for the wedding. It is particularly meaningful if this piece of jewelry belonged to his mother or another dear relative. The bride may give the groom a dated and inscribed watch, a pair of cuff links, or even a set of luggage in which to set off on your honeymoon together.

The Duties of Your Attendants

Maid of Honor

Helps with prewedding plans and errands.

Hosts bridal shower.

Arranges and pays for fitting of her dress.

Selects bridal gift to come from bridesmaids.

Supervises bridesmaids before ceremony.

Helps bride dress before wedding.

Holds bridal bouquet and groom's ring during ceremony; straightens bridal train and adjusts veil; gives bride back her bouquet before recessional.

Signs wedding certificate as a legal witness.

Stands in receiving line.

Helps bride change into going-away costume.

Bridesmaids

Participate in bridal shower and wedding parties.

Arrange and pay for fitting for their dresses.

Precede the bride down the aisle and follow her out.

Act as informal hostesses at reception.

Best Man

Helps groom with arrangements for bachelor dinner and honeymoon.

Assists groom in dressing for ceremony and packing for honeymoon.

Supervises other ushers, making sure they come for fittings and know what their jobs are during the ceremony.

Signs marriage license and holds clergy fee until after ceremony when he presents it.

Offers first toast at reception, helps groom dress for going away. Brings car around to door for getaway.

Ushers

Head usher—supervises other ushers during the ceremony.

Participate in bachelors' party and wedding festivities.

Arrange for fitting of their outfits and pay for rental.

Arrive at wedding one hour early to help escort guests to their seats.

Escort bridesmaids down the aisle after the ceremony.

Act as informal hosts and escorts during reception.

Junior Attendants

Junior ushers—assist ushers.

Junior bridesmaids—march in procession and recession; participate in showers and parties.

Ring bearer—carries ring in procession.

Flower girl—scatters paper petals down aisle preceding bride.

Train bearer—supports bridal train behind bride during procession and recession.

Mother of the Bride

Assists bride and groom in planning and carrying out wedding— from clothing for all the members to ceremony and reception.

May entertain out of town guests on evening of a morning wedding or for brunch or lunch the day after an evening wedding.

Official hostess at reception, greeting guests first in the receiving line.

Father of the Bride

Assists in planning wedding and traditionally pays most of the bills (see Chapter 3).

Escorts bride down the aisle and gives her away at the altar.

Acts as official host at the reception.

Groom's Parents

Act as consultants during planning stages.

Traditionally host rehearsal dinner.

Can participate in honeymoon plans and expenses.

Other Members of the Family and Close Friends

Can host parties in bridal couple's honor.

Give toasts during all the festivities.

Run errands as requested.

If unmarried, should participate in the tossing of the garter and bouquet.

Can help decorate the getaway car.

Chapter 6
A Trousseau for You and Your Groom

Tradition

Years ago a bride's trousseau included not only a new wardrobe, from undergarments to hats, but linens as well. We'll deal with linens in the wedding gifts chapter and just consider clothes, both yours and his, in our modern trousseau.

Think of your trousseau as the wardrobe you hope to build upon for years to come. This is your opportunity to start a new wardrobe with your new life. And, just as you have done when planning your wedding ensemble, your new wardrobe plan must take your color season, life style, clothing personality, and budget into account. You want each clothing piece to reflect you in the best possible light.

Since you are starting a new life, it's a good time to look at what you have. I once worked with a bride-to-be who had a dress in every imaginable color, with shoes and bags to match. That is not a wardrobe. It's a waste of money. If you are on a limited budget, discipline yourself and plan what you can spend and on what. Even if your budget is unlimited, you will want to get your money's worth from everything you buy. You don't want to clutter your closet with a blouse that only goes with one suit or a pair of shoes that work with just one pair of pants.

Let's open your closet door, pull out all the old, bent wire hangers and throw them away. Next dig back into the far corners and pull out all those clothes that date back to high school and haven't been worn since. If they are out of fashion or out of your color season, give them away with the wire hangers right now. Call the Goodwill or the Salvation Army and give those old clothes a chance to do someone some good.

Next, organize the remaining clothes by color. A portable clothes or coat rack is a wonderful tool for wardrobe organization. Hang your clothes on it by predominant colors, even in prints and patterned clothing. Notice color "themes" you have intuitively gathered over the years. Are you a Winter with a lot of red in your wardrobe? A Summer who has a passion for blue? An Autumn who can't stay away from brown? A Spring who is into yellow? Perhaps that dominant color is the key to your revitalized wardrobe. It could be the color you use to create different outfits from, to mix and match the various pieces you assemble.

Take all the clothing in this favorite color or colors and look at what items you have. Are all or any of them suitable for your new lifestyle? Are they appropriate for work or play? Do they fit? Are they the right length? Do they need mending? Sort them into piles for action and begin to fill in the Wardrobe Planning Chart . . .

Current Wardrobe Planning Chart

Clothing Items	Color	Fabric	Use
Coats			
Dress			
Casual			
Dresses			
Skirts			

Clothing Items	Color	Fabric	Use
Blouses			
Sweaters			
Jackets			
Shoes			
Sports clothes			
Bags			

What's Missing?

Now you know what you have. Let's think about what you'll need for the wedding festivities, your honeymoon, and your life after the wedding.

First of all, what parties do you anticipate your friends and family will be giving you and your groom? Will you need evening clothes, cocktail dresses, dinner ensembles? Will you have use for them after the wedding? How much do you have to invest?

Next, your honeymoon. Where and when are the important questions. Will you be doing a lot of sightseeing and need comfortable shoes and easy-to-wash, no iron fabrics? Or will you be lying on the beach and dancing the night away? Will you be away for a weekend, for a month?

What about your "going away" outfit? Will you be leaving for your honeymoon right after the wedding? Or will you be leaving later and going to a warmer or colder climate?

Then, what will you be doing after all the festivities are over and you and your groom have returned from your honeymoon? Will you be working in an office, or puttering around your new apartment? What clothes will you need to carry on your new life?

Answer these questions, then fill in this chart...

What I Need

Wedding Activities	Clothing Items	Color	Fabric
Parties			
Showers			

Wedding Activities	Clothing Items	Color	Fabric
Other Events			
Honeymoon			
Going Away Costume			
Travel			
Sports			

Colors for Brides

Wedding Activities	Clothing Items	Color	Fabric
Evening			
After the Wedding			
Work			
Entertaining			
Sports			

A Trousseau for You and Your Groom

Wedding Activities	Clothing Items	Color	Fabric
Other			
Lingerie			
Accessories			

Now combine your two lists. Put "What I Have" into "What I Need" and you'll see the clothing items you must invest in to build the wardrobe you want for this next big phase of your life.

Your Color Season

Turn to your seasonal palette of colors. How many of the items you've saved are in your colors? If a clothing piece isn't in your palette, can it be "decorated" with a scarf or is it worn away from your face? Then save it. If not, consider giving it to a friend whose color it is.

Look for predominant color combinations. Do you seem to favor one or two colors over others? Do the clothing pieces in these colors mix and match to make other outfits? What other pieces could you add in these predominant colors to make complete outfits: blouses, a jacket, another skirt, a pair of pants, a sweater? Sometimes one major purchase like a jacket in one of your neutral colors will pull many clothing items together into finished outfits. That's the magic of color.

Your Clothing Personality and Lifestyle

Not surprisingly, the formality of the wedding you have chosen says much about your clothing personality. So it seems even more appropriate to take it into consideration when planning the wardrobe that must meet all the requirements of your lifestyle.

The ultraformal dramatic bride probably looks forward to a life full of parties and evening occasions. She may work in a profession that demands high fashion. Her relaxation time may be spent in museums rather than ball parks. She will need a more formal wardrobe with evening and work clothes predominating. On a strict budget, she is the woman who should scrimp to buy one very expensive, very high-quality item that mixes and matches with the other expensive, high-quality items in her wardrobe. The high fashion, at least in the beginning, will have to come from her accessories, which reflect her dramatic, fast-paced personality.

If you are a dramatic Winter, start your wardrobe with a skirt and jacket in black, red, or white. Add blouses in those same colors and a silk dress that can be worn with the jacket and you have a splendid daytime wardrobe for the winter months. In the summer, if you are a true dramatic, you'll wear nothing but black and white in the city or all white accented with some dynamite colors from your palette for resort wear. Your best fabrics are satin, brocade, metallics, wool, linen, and velvet. Your best prints are geometrics, contrasting stripes, and bold paisleys.

The formal classic bride is much more traditional. Her lifestyle more conducive to occasions where classic style is more appropriate than the latest fad. She probably works in a less glamorous, more traditional profession, where knowledge not flair is most respected. She, too, should purchase one expensive item per season in the beginning, building up a classic mix-and-match-forever wardrobe.

If you are a classic Summer, start with a light-to-medium gray soft straight skirt with a shawl-collared jacket. Add a pair of pleated trousers, several tailored tie- or jabot-necked blouses in your pinks and plums, classic gray pumps and bag, and pearls, and you are set for daytime. In the warmer months, try an off-white skirt, jacket, and pleated trousers, mixed with your pastels and off-white shoes and hose. Your best fabrics are silk or wool crepe, wool flannel and jersey, cashmere, cotton or cotton blends, and silk shantung. Your best patterns are small, evenly spaced stripes, geometric designs, quiet paisleys, and small polka dots.

The semiformal romantic bride is the woman who can go either way with versatility. She can dress up for a formal evening, but prefers the more casual lifestyle. She chooses dresses over suits, femininity rather than formality. If she wears a suit at all, it will be a fitted dressmaker suit, or a silk dress with a fitted jacket. She likes to show off her small waist with full skirts and wide belts. Her blouses are always silk with ruffles or bows and lace. She likes shoes with open toes and heels. This romantic look is good for the creative career she has been attracted to, where flowing lines are appreciated in fashion and on paper.

If you are a romantic Spring, build your wardrobe around light warm beiges or light warm browns to mix with your peach and apricot blouses and dresses. Your shoes should be a light warm brown, your jewelry pearls and gold. During the warmer months, invest in an ivory silk jacket, skirt, and soft pleated trousers to wear with your pinks, peaches, periwinkles, and aquas, and ivory shoes and hose. Silks, lace, velvets, soft wools, angora, jersey, satin, chiffon, and handkerchief linens are your best fabrics. Your best prints are flowers and polka dots.

The informal natural bride looks for easy silhouettes—unconstructed jackets, fabrics with a casual matte finish, leather belts, millions of sweaters and lots of pants and comfortable skirts and blouses, shirtdresses rather than suits, sweaters rather than jackets. She likes flat and low-heeled shoes of fine leather or canvas. She has most likely been attracted to a profession where she can work outdoors or with people, not paper. She needs comfortable, on-the-move clothes and very little evening wear.

If you are an Autumn, your basic wardrobe should include beiges, browns, glen plaids, shadow checks, houndstooth wools, small checks and stripes—all blended and muted with little contrast. For semiformal business occasions, start with a solid skirt and jacket that you can wear with a paisley blouse and shawl, natural leather shoulder bag, medium-heeled pumps, gold chain, and earrings. In the summer, an oyster linen suit with matching pants is your best investment. Wear it with your teals, turquoises, and dusty corals, ivory jewelry or wooden beads, and bone-colored shoes. Woven textures such as linen and tweed, gabardine, raw silk, leather, cotton velvet, wool flannel, camel's hair, suede, cotton, and velveteen are your best fabrics. Your best patterns are plaids, checks, paisleys, and natural motifs.

Your Body Type

As you know, we advise dressing to reflect your clothing personality and color season rather than body type. But just as you did with your wedding dress, emphasize the positive, downplay the negative. If you have heavy legs, don't wear light-colored hosiery and flat shoes. Slip into matte or dark hosiery with low heels or even high heels to slim your legs and add a longer line to your entire body silhouette. Keep skirts below the knee or just above it, and if you are a little heavy, make them A-line or straight with a loose top. Invest in well-cut, quality fabric pants with a straight-leg cut and plenty of room.

If you are tall, broad-shouldered and long-legged, a jacket—single or double-breasted, with notched lapels, and cut straight or semi-fitted—will look great on you. Most jackets are too long for the average woman.

If your shoulders are too narrow, use fasten-on shoulder pads under blouses, sweaters, and dresses. Choose ruffles for sleeveless gowns. The shawl-collared jacket—single buttoned or wrapped with a sash—is wonderful on you, as is the classic Chanel jacket. If your arms are too skinny, don't wear tight-fitting sleeves. For heavy arms, the same goes. Don't squeeze them into tight sleeves. Loose-fitting sleeves and a low-cut neckline keep everything in proportion.

If your bust is big, be sure to invest in a good support bra. Avoid ruffled necklines and tightly cinched waists. Wear open-throated blouses and shirts with scooped or square necklines. A little cleavage can be pretty. If your bust is small, a lightly-padded bra and loose-fitting tops look best.

If your waist is small, show it off with a graceful circular skirt made out of a lightweight fabric. If your hips and waist are pretty much in a straight line, choose a pleated skirt. The pleats will fall straight down, just as they should. You also look good in a wrap skirt. Straight skirts are best on slender women, perfectly fitted A-lines on larger ones. But the gently gathered dirndl is becoming to everyone.

The trick is balance. If one part of you is too small, wear loose-fitting or brightly-colored clothing there. If another is too large, wear darker colored, straighter lines there. And enhance whatever is your beauty feature. If it's your hair, arrange it so everyone notices it first. If it's your face, wear the colors that bring it out. If it's your hands, decorate them with lovely jewelry and nail polish. If it's your legs, wear skirt lengths, hosiery, and shoes that emphasize their shapeliness.

The Wardrobe for All Seasons

You don't need a huge wardrobe, you need a good one, one that is versatile and well-made. Be a smart investor, buy one quality item per season in colors that complement and coordinate with the rest of your wardrobe. Though tempting, don't buy a lot of inexpensive, faddish clothes you'll throw away at the end of the season. Now is the time to begin building a wardrobe that reflects you at your best.

Suits and Blouses. A suit doesn't have to consist of a matching skirt and jacket. It can be any three pieces, two of which match. For instance, a blouse and skirt could match and be worn with a different jacket. A blouse and jacket could match and be worn with a different skirt. Or, the skirt and jacket could match and be worn with a different blouse.

Start with two solid-colored suits in colors that can be mixed to make four different outfits: each suit, plus a mix of the two different jackets and skirts. Or, you can buy four solid pieces: two jackets, two skirts or trousers, or one skirt and one pair of trousers. These four pieces with different blouses, sweaters, and tops can become countless outfits. Solid colors are easy to begin with; but remember that when any two pieces are worn together, they must create the correct contrast for your coloring. The contrast for Winters should be cool and sharp; for Springs, warm and bright; for Summers, cool and soft; and for Autumns, warm and muted. Be sure to use the colors in your palette or this trick won't work.

If you need more business outfits, start with two neutrals from your palette, or a neutral and a color. The texture and weight of the fabric must be compatible. For instance, lightweight wools can be worn with silk. Silk can be worn with linen. Linen can be worn with fine cotton. You can mix patterns and textures, but do it carefully. A tweed skirt should be worn with a solid blouse. A soft wool flannel can be mixed with a tweed and a soft tweed goes with velvet.

After you have selected your four basic solid-colored pieces, start looking for tops to go with them. You can start with three plain tops that mix and match. The shirt/blouse with concealed buttons and a small-to-medium collar is a classic. The shawl-collared blouse flatters most women, and a tie-necked blouse will soften your tailored suit and look great with trousers. Then look for a two-piece print dress and a one-piece solid dress that you can wear with the two jackets. The shirtdress is probably the most versatile of dresses and it looks good on everyone. There are many variations, try them on and choose the one that is best for you. The two-piece print can be worn with a plain wool jacket or be dressed up with a velvet jacket.

The best fabrics for blouses are silk, cotton, and linen. If the two pieces you are wearing are different colors, wear an accessory at your neck—a scarf or necklace—that is the same color as the skirt or a pattern the includes both colors.

Your working wardrobe will work for several seasons of the year if you choose pieces that are moderate in style and fabric. Avoid highly stylized jackets, very narrow or very wide lapels, very full or very straight skirts, very wide or very tapered pants. Depending on where you live, you may need both cold and warm weather outfits. In most parts of this country, you can wear fabrics of lightweight wool or wool blends combined with silk blouses and dresses most of the year. If you live in a warmer area, silk, linen and linen blends will work all year round.

Shoes. Your shoes should match your skirt or your hair. A good guide is to wear light-to-medium shoes with light suits; medium-to-dark shoes with mid-tones; and dark shoes with dark colors. The pump is the most basic shoe shape, and there are variations that flatter all of us. Pumps with low, stacked heels look good with pants. Pumps with high, slender heels are dressier. The pump is a great business shoe. Flats are the casual shoe for your pants, but a cropped boot is the casual shoe for an Autumn natural. A skirt boot with a slim foot and graceful heel is good on everyone else.

Winters, your shoes should be black, white, bone, or navy. Summers, slip into bone, gray, light navy, and rose brown. Autumns, you need to choose from ivory, bone, warm beige, light brown or dark brown. Springs float along in ivory, beige, light gray, light navy, or light brown shoes.

Accessories. The basic belt is fairly narrow with a covered buckle. If you choose a belt with a metal buckle, it should be the metal of your season so that it will go with your clothes and jewelry. There are also sashes and cummerbunds with no buckles to worry about. Cummerbunds come in long, wide fabric or even soft leather that can be wrapped and twisted around your waist in a number of interesting ways.

You'll need two good leather bags: a roomy rectangular bag and a slim envelope that can be slipped inside. These two bags should go together, and go with your shoes.

To decorate your neck, you'll want an assortment of scarves that complement your business outfits: one shawl, one square scarf, and one oblong that can be used as a tie sash.

To wrap up your wardrobe on those colder, wetter days, invest in a good, unlined raincoat and an unlined wool coat that will fit over your suits. I recommend your coats be unlined so that they are weightless and seasonless. Just wear more underneath them when it is colder.

Lingerie. If you've never cared about it before, now is the time to start. There are so many lovely undergarments to choose from and you'll need nightgowns or pajamas, a robe, panties, bras, and slips. Use your palette and your knowledge of your best fabrics and patterns to help you put together this intimate wardrobe. If you are on a limited budget, buy undergarments in a nude shade closest to your skin color. Nude, not white, works under everything.

Springs, your romantic sleepwear should be in ivory, peach, warm pink, periwinkle, or aqua. Summers, yours should be off-white, pink, blue, or lavender. Autumns, slip into warm beige, apricot, or gold. Winters, slither into white, black, icy pink, blue, or violet, or vivid jewel tones.

Hosiery. Don't forget your legs! Your hosiery should help pull each outfit together. Here is a summary of the best colors for each season.

Winters	Summers	Autumns	Springs
rose beige	rose beige	golden beige	light golden beige
taupe beige	grayed navy	golden brown	light navy
white	light gray	ivory	ivory
black	rose brown		nude
gray	bone		
navy			

Here is a summary of the fabrics and prints that are best for each of the clothing personalities. In general, straight lines are for dramatic and classic types; rounded shapes, such as polka dots, for romantics and the small ingenue types. Square shapes, such as checks and plaids, are best for naturals and small gamins.

Lingerie

If you've never cared about it before, you should now. If you're a classic or romantic, you'll want at least one long nightdress and peignoir; if you're a natural, a pair of silk pajamas. If you're a Winter, you'll want pieces you can combine in different ways: a long nightdress, with matching long or short kimono, pajama pants and camisole top.

A Trousseau for You and Your Groom

Colors for Brides

Dramatics

Bold, contrasting prints with widely-spaced and geometric patterns or solids, on the most formal and extreme in fabrics.

Prints
geometrics,
contrasting stripes,
bold paisleys

Fabrics
satin, brocade, velvet,
metallics, wool, and
linen

Classics

Prints which are closely spaced and solids or light-to-medium weight fabrics with a matte or soft sheen finish.

Prints
small evenly-spaced stripes,
small geometric designs,
small, evenly-spaced
paisleys

Fabrics
silk, wool crepe, wool
flannel and jersey, cashmere,
cotton and cotton blends,
peau de soie, silk shantung

Naturals

Prints with medium to large blended patterns, with matte finishes and textures.

Prints
plaids, checks,
paisleys,
natural motifs such as
animal prints

Fabrics
raw silk, linen, tweed,
gabardine, flannel, jersey,
and velvet

Romantics

Soft but sophisticated prints on soft, lustrous fabrics which drape easily.

Prints
flowers, polka dots

Fabrics
silk, chiffon, soft wool,
angora, soft jersey, satin,
velvet and lace

Makeup

The chart below will help you determine which daily makeup colors will enhance your season and your style. On your wedding day, you'll want to use the romantic colors and wear a pink or peach lipstick from your palette. On that day of days, you want to look your softest and most beguiling. If you are a Winter, however, who has planned a red and white Christmas wedding or an Autumn who has selected deep Renaissance colors, wear a lipstick to complement your scheme.

Using this guide for lipstick colors, you can develop different schemes to coordinate with your clothes. Blush should match lipstick color, shadows should complement eyes and clothes as well as coordinate with lipstick and blush.

Suggestions for Makeup Color Schemes

	Dramatic	Classic	Romantic	Natural
Winter	Scarlet Magenta Fuschia	Rose Wine Plum	Hot Pink	Gloss or Stain
Summer	Rosy Red	Soft Rose Soft Raspberry Soft Plum	True Pink Rose Pink Mauve Pink	Gloss or Stain
Spring	Poppy Red Cherry Red	Coral Rose	Warm Pink Peach Pink Coral Pink	Gloss or Stain
Autumn	Tomato Red Brick Red	Bronze Rose Amber Rose	Apricot Peach Coffee	Gloss or Stain

Always apply a color perfection cream first, dotted gently on your face then blended with a sponge. Olive or sallow skin, needs a violet-tinted cream. Ruddy skins can be toned down with green-tinted cream. Cover blue or violet areas around your eyes with a yellow-tinted cream.

Ask your consultant to help you put together a makeup "wardrobe" or send for our list in the back of the book. Your consultant can be especially helpful in coordinating your makeup for your bridal portrait.

Haircolor

Suggestions for Your Season and Style

Ask your hairdresser to help you become a little more Winter, Summer, Spring or Autumn. The following chart can be used as a guide.

	Dramatic	Classic	Romantic	Natural
Winter	Platinum Blonde Jet Black	Dark Ash Brown	Black Black-brown	Medium–to–Dark Brown with high-lights
Summer	Lightest Ash Blonde Frosted	Light–to–medium Ash Blonde	Light Ash Blonde	Light Ash Brown with Ash Blonde streaks
Spring	Bright Yellow Blonde	Light–to–medium Flaxen Blonde	Yellow Blonde Red Blonde	Light Golden Brown with Golden Blonde streaks
Autumn	Fiery Red	Medium–to–Dark Golden Blonde	Honey Auburn	Medium–to–Dark Golden Brown with Golden Blonde highlights

The Dramatic Face

Emphasize your eyes and lips by using the light and dark colors from your palette and a matte finish foundation one or two shades lighter than your skin. Keep your hair sleek, either worn up in a chignon or down.

Begin with a color perfection cream to cover flaws. Apply your foundation with a sponge. Brush your eyebrows into an arch with cake eyebrow powder. Line your upper and lower eyelids with pencil. Apply a lighter shade of shadow on your lids, then line the crease above your eyelid with eyeshadow. Apply mascara. Dust on translucent or pearlized powder. Add a small amount of blush from your hairline down to the outer rim of your iris. Line your lips with pencil, apply your lipstick, and add gloss.

The Classic Face

Emphasize your eyes, cheeks, and lips equally. Use a matte finish foundation and medium, opaque colors from your palette. Your hair should be soft, worn either in a pageboy or upswept in a French twist or roll.

Begin with a color perfection cream to cover flaws. Apply foundation that is one shade lighter than your skin with a sponge. Brush your eyebrows into a classic arch with cake eyebrow powder. Apply highlighter under the full length of your brow. Eyeshadow should be applied to your lids and the crease above your eyelid. Dot cream blush on the hollows under your cheeks. Then dust your face with a translucent powder, applying powder blush under your cheek bones. Apply mascara. Line your lips with a pencil then apply your lipstick. Do not use gloss.

The Natural Face

Emphasize your eyes and eyebrows, using your medium-to-dark colors and medium foundation shade to give you that suntanned look. Wear your hair long, unset, and full or short and windblown.

As with all the other looks, begin with a color perfection cream to cover skin flaws. Apply your foundation with a face sponge. Then brush your eyebrows with a cake eyebrow powder into a straight line, right across to the underbrow so that your eyebrows appear dark and thick. Apply eyeshadow from your lashes to your brows. Apply blush cheek-to-cheek across your nose and a light dab to your forehead and chin to give you a sunkissed look. Outline your lips with a lip pencil, and gloss or stain them.

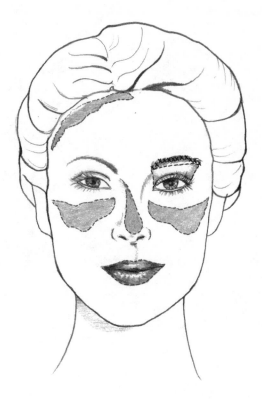

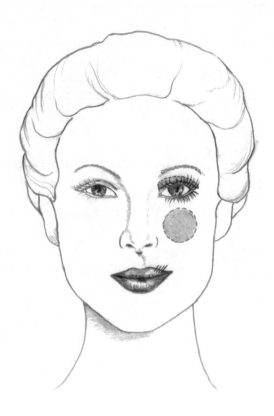

The Romantic Face

Your makeup should softly emphasize all your facial features with light–to–medium sheer colors. Your complexion should look creamy with a dewy finish. Wear your hair long and softly curled or piled high with escaping curls and tendrils.

Begin your makeup application by covering any skin flaws with concealer. Apply a sheer foundation, blending with a face sponge. Brush your eyebrows into a rounded arch using cake eyebrow powder. Draw a wide-domed line around your eyes with a sheer neutral crayon, then gently smudge to blur the edges and give you a doe-eyed appearance. Apply your eyeshadow and mascara to the top and bottom lashes, using more mascara in the middle to center your lashes and give you a wide-eyed look. Apply cream blush to the apple of each cheek, blending well with a sponge. Dust your face lightly with translucent powder. Then apply a sheer lipstick. Pat your face with a dampened sponge to give you a dewy look.

A Trousseau for You and Your Groom

Your Groom - Time to Check Out His Closet

Many men have not yet heard about wardrobe building. They buy their clothes one piece at a time with no thought of coordinating. But there are ways they can assemble a well-tailored wardrobe that make them look as good as they know they are.

If your man has been out in the working world, he has probably collected some business suits, shirts, ties, and shoes. But maybe you can help him put them all together in your new closets.

Men have a clothing personality, just as women do. If your groom readily agreed to an ultraformal wedding, he probably has the same dramatic flair that you do. He is a sophisticated type who would rather play tennis than toss a football. He may tend toward high-fashion styles, as you do, and prefer expensive fabric, like silks, wools, cottons, and linen (everything that needs ironing!).

The formal groom is a little more traditional, just like his bride. He prefers classic, conservative clothing, very well tailored in natural fibers and patterns—wools, cottons, and silks, tweeds, and broadcloth. You may find him playing tennis with his ultraformal friend, but he will always be in white.

Your semiformal man has a dash of romance and adventure. He can be formal or informal, enjoying the fun of dressing up as much as jumping into a pair of shorts for a vigorous game of volleyball on the beach. His wardrobe will be full of the clothes he has bought over the years to try out each new sport as he discovers it. His will be the closet that really needs weeding. He may never have bothered to throw anything away in his haste to move on to the next adventure.

The informal guy is as natural as they come. You'll have a hard time getting him into a suit at all, but he'll look great in it when you do. He's a relaxed, easygoing kind of outdoors man, who would rather climb a mountain than work his way up the corporate ladder. His wardrobe will need your help in adding a tiny bit of formality, even if it is only a dark business suit, a good blazer, and slacks.

His Basics

Your groom should fill in similar "What I Have" and "What I Need" charts, leaving off the lingerie and skirts, of course, and substituting suits. He should also have a nice robe and pajamas for your honeymoon trip as well as the appropriate sports equipment. Here is his chart . . .

Current Wardrobe Planning Chart

Clothing Items	Color	Fabric	Use
Coats			
Dress			
Casual			
Suits			
Shirts			
Sweaters			
Jackets			
Sports			
Blazers			

Clothing Items	Color	Fabric	Use
Shoes			
Sports clothes			
Evening clothes			
Leisure Wear			

Your man's sports and leisure wear should be as high in quality as his business gear. Exact fit is even more important when he is sporting bolder colors and patterns. Solids, plaids, and checks are best. Dots, stripes, and busy multi-directional patterns can be too much for many men. Balance bright or deep colors with sweaters and solid pants in neutral colors and softer textures.

If you are going on a Caribbean honeymoon, besides sporting equipment, your sophisticated Winter man will need informal, leisure outfits. A navy blazer with silver buttons, white pants, white shirt, burgundy and navy tie or a white jacket and navy pants, white shirt, and burgundy and navy tie are great nonbusiness combinations for him.

Your classic Summer guy can also sport a navy blazer with silver-toned buttons, but his pants should be off-white, and his shirt off-white or pastel—pink, blue, or yellow—worn with a pink and navy, blue and navy, or yellow and navy tie, depending on his shirt. He can also go for an off-white jacket, navy pants, pastel shirt and tie in warmer times or warmer places.

Your rugged Autumn man should wear a cream jacket and chocolate pants with a peach or aqua shirt, and peach and chocolate, or aqua and chocolate tie. A redhead might go for a navy blazer with cream pants, a light gold shirt, and gold and navy tie.

Your dashing Spring fellow should wear a navy blazer with gold-colored buttons, cream-colored pants, a peach, blue, or cream shirt, and a peach and navy, blue and navy, or cream and navy tie.

When He Means Business

If your guy needs your help organizing a new business wardrobe, here are some suggestions, according to season.

The Winter Man

- A navy suit, white shirt, navy and burgundy, or solid burgundy tie.

- A medium or dark gray solid or pinstripe suit with a white shirt, and gray and burgundy tie; or with a blue shirt, a blue and navy, or blue and black tie.

- A gray-blue glen plaid suit, with a blue button-down collar shirt, and a medium blue and navy tie.

- A tan poplin suit with a blue button-down collar shirt and blue and navy tie.

The Summer Man

- A navy suit, white shirt, light blue and medium blue tie.

- A blue-gray suit, blue shirt, medium blue, gray, and navy tie.

- A gray-blue glen plaid suit, blue button-down shirt, and medium blue-gray and navy tie.
- A tan poplin suit with pink button-down shirt and off white, pink and navy tie.

The Spring Man

- A navy suit, ivory shirt, and cream and navy tie.
- A medium gray suit, gray or blue shirt, and a blue and navy tie.
- A beige suit with cream or blue shirt, and cream and navy, or navy and blue tie.
- A tan poplin suit with a blue button-down shirt, and blue and navy tie; or an ivory button-down shirt and ivory and navy tie.

The Autumn Man

- A dark chocolate brown suit, ivory shirt, and ivory, beige and brown tie.
- A medium beige solid-colored suit, light beige or cream shirt and beige, peach, and brown or beige, aqua, and brown tie.
- A tan poplin suit with aqua shirt and beige and aqua tie, or a peach shirt with beige and peach tie.
- An olive drab poplin suit with aqua shirt and olive, aqua, and cream tie.

You'll notice that all the seasons can wear the tan poplin suit and the navy blazer. When these are worn with their own colored or white shirts and ties, they look good on everyone.

The basic business suit jacket comes with one, two, three, or four buttons. The most becoming to the majority of men is the two-button jacket. The three-button is considered Ivy League, and only the middle button should be closed. Always keep two-button and four-button double-breasted jackets closed. Buttons should match the color of the suit, and metal buttons are for blazers only. Sleeve buttons are only truly functional on very expensive custom-tailored suits.

Suit or jacket lapels can be either notched, semi-notched, peaked, or semi-peaked. The notched collar is the classic style and will withstand the vagaries of fashion. Classic Summers and natural Autumns look best in the notched collar. The semi-peaked collar is often found on a high fashion suit, best on the sophisticated Winter or adventurous Spring.

Men's pants come straight, tapered, or flared with pleated or plain tops. Flared pants should never be worn for business. Pockets are either side-seam or slashed, and cuffs are optional. The tall classic man wears cuffs well. Shorter men do not.

A man's vest should fit like his second skin. It should be long enough to cover his waistband and should barely show above his lapels when his jacket is buttoned. The bottom button is never closed.

A man should wear his suit, it should not wear him. Whether he chooses the natural-shouldered, American/British, European, or Athletic cut, it should fit him. The American/British cut suit is the classic. With its lightly padded shoulders, slightly tapered waist, side or center vents of not more than 8 inches, lapel no wider than half the distance between the collar and the shoulder, and straight-legged, uncuffed pants, it never goes out of fashion, especially when made from natural fibers like wool, silk, cotton, and linen.

Neckties should end at the top of his belt. The classic width is 2¾ inches to 3½ inches. The best ties for business are *rep* (diagonal stripes in varying widths), *club* (small, evenly spaced motifs on a solid background), and *Ivy League* (very small motifs on a solid background). For weekends and informal times, when he needs to wear a tie, the knitted, challis, plaid, or print tie is fine. A four-in-hand knotted tie should be worn with all shirts—whether straight, round, button-down, or pinned collar. A Windsor knot goes with a spread-collar shirt. One-half inch of cuff should show below his sleeve.

The best shirt colors for business are in the lightest range of his palette. Striped shirts are also acceptable, but the closer and finer the stripe and the fewer the colors, the more authoritative the look. A fine box plaid is all right, but if he would even consider wearing it as a sports shirt, he shouldn't wear it to the office.

Over the calf is the *only* length of hose he should wear in business. They should be the same color as his suit or shoes.Business shoes are brown or black wing tip or plain lace. Avoid patent leather.

Every man should own a beige raincoat. His overcoat can be solid beige, gray, or camel depending on his season.

A few tips on accessories . . .

A Trousseau for You and Your Groom

- Never wear colored handkerchiefs to the office.

- His billfold and briefcase should be leather.

- Use a gold or silver pen and pencil.

- Keep cuff links small-to-medium, depending on his size, and gold or silver, depending on his season.

- Never combine two patterns that go in opposite directions.

- Never wear more than two patterns at one time.

- Wear a solid shirt and a non-directional tie with a plaid suit.

- Wear a rep tie with a pinstripe suit, only if the pattern is subtle.

- If he has a long, angular face or is very tall and thin, he should avoid vertical stripes. Rep ties, long designs, narrow ties, and jackets that are too long will make him look too tall.

- If he is heavy or short, vertical stripes will make him look taller. Avoid heavy or bulky fabrics or clothes that are too form-fitting.

- If he is large and imposing, he can wear lighter, more friendly colors to avoid looking too aggressive.

- If he is slight, he should wear darker colors, as long as they are not exaggerated. A short haircut, moustache, and dark rimmed glasses will also add maturity and stature.

Packing It All In

You and your groom should plan for a handsome set of luggage to start your traveling days together. Luggage can be included on your list of wedding gifts if you don't already have a nice set. You must choose between molded hard-side luggage, which is difficult to store and heavier to carry but more durable, and soft-side luggage, which can be more difficult to pack but is lighter and easier to carry. The three basic pieces are the large Pullman which is 29 to 30 inches long, the medium Pullman which is 26 inches long, and the carry-on which fits under the seat in the airplane. You may also want a hanging garment bag which will come in handy for business travel later in your lives. Decide who is going to have what suitcase. If you are leaving right from the reception, you'll have to be packed ahead of time.

The basics of packing are:

- Put all non-crushable items like shoes, hair dryer, and bags on the bottom of the suitcase.

- Hang each clothing item that might wrinkle on a thin hanger, cover it with a plastic bag, and fold it in three. Place it carefully in suitcase. Now it won't wrinkle and it's ready to pull out and hang up when you get to your destination.

- Put other garments like sweaters and underwear in plastic bags.

- Don't pack aerosol cans, nail polish, and jewelry in your suitcase. Carry it in your airplane bag or purse with your airline tickets, passport, credit cards, checkbook, and other important papers you want right with you at all times.

Chapter 7
Planning the Ceremony

The First Visit to Your Clergy

Now is the time to contact that very important person who will perform your marriage ceremony. As soon as you decide you want to be married, you and your fiance should make an appointment to discuss the service with your clergymember and to tour the facilities. Most rabbis, priests, and ministers will want to have at least one premarital counseling session to review your legal and religious obligations. They will also want to prepare you spiritually for marriage, a very sacred part of any religion, and discuss your plans for the future together.

This will be your time to review the marriage service and talk over the meaning of the words. If you have decided that you want to write your own service or add some elements (songs, poems, readings), discuss it at this meeting. Some clergymembers are not permitted to deviate from the prescribed marriage service. Others will be able to help you with examples of vows, psalms, and songs other couples have used under his or her auspices. Work out all the details with your priest, rabbi, or minister and confirm the date and time for the ceremony.

Then take a tour of the facilities. Note the colors of the walls, rugs, windows, altar hangings, wood tones of pews, pillars, and moldings. Is it large or small, modern or traditional, formal or informal? Is the setting elaborate or simple? Take it all in. Take pictures if you'll need to remember a detail at a later date. These will be useful for your floral designer who may be unfamiliar with the layout.

If you have decided to be married at a club or hotel, visit these facilities right away. Tour the rooms you will be using and note the colors and decor. Confirm the date and time. You may be required to sign a contract and put down a deposit, particularly if you are having a catered reception in the same place. Local custom may play an important part in your plans. What is formal in one part of the country may not be in another. Be sure you know what traditions are expected in your area. In smaller towns you may not be able to find all the elements you need for a formal wedding close at hand and will have to plan well in advance to order by mail or purchase in the big city and bring home with you.

Long-distance planning can also cause problems. If you live in one place and the wedding is in another, start your plans early. A bridal consultant in your wedding town would be a tremendous help to you and your family. Look for package deals for your reception site that include food, flowers, and music in one price. Visit home several times before the wedding to check on the arrangements, confirm contracts and rentals by phone more than once. Be certain you know the legal requirements in the area for marriage license, blood test, and so forth. Register your wedding gift selections in stores in your wedding town and plan how you will get them home with you after the festivities. Again, a bridal consultant can be a big help. Check with the Association of Bridal Consultants for the names of members in the town where you will be married. They can help you launch your long distance wedding.

Second Weddings

If you are taking a second chance on love, there are special considerations to keep in mind. The ceremony should be simple and dignified—no great hoopla, please. Keep it simple, but make it happy. Forget the fancy engraved invitations, but do ask your father to give you away if you wish. Or dispense with this part of the ceremony altogether. You may walk in alone, or even with your mother. Plan the wedding for a church, club, or your home; and by all means, ask your best friend to be your maid or matron of honor and include your other favorites as your bridesmaids, even your own children when appropriate. Find the most beautiful dress—in your own white—but go for the semiformal or informal, despite your dramatic tendencies. Be lavish with flowers if you want. Your bridegroom should certainly have his best friend attend him. If this is his second wedding—but only your first—conduct your wedding as you would like it, simple but elegant. Wear your white wedding gown.

If this is your second marriage, however, or you are a more mature bride, look for that elegant white suit or dress. Your dress need not even be white. One of the light colors or neutrals from your palette will always look good. Mid-calf or long dresses are always appropriate for the more formal second wedding, knee length for the informal. Wear a hat or some other headpiece, but avoid the veil, which is a symbol of virginity.

Simple elegance is the byword, especially if you have decided upon a civil ceremony. Here you would certainly choose a handsome street-length dress or suit. A full-of-fun wedding breakfast with all your friends should follow.

Have your reception or a party for your friends at a later date be the big celebration. The second wedding should be happy but sedate.

The Guest List

As soon as you know where and when you will be married, what your budget is, and how formal the festivities will be, it is time to make up the wedding list. Invitations must be ordered three-to-four months ahead, and mailed to arrive one month ahead, so begin collecting names and addresses right away.

When you have determined the number of people you will be able to include in the ceremony and the reception, let your fiance and his family know exactly how many guests they can invite and when you will need their names and addresses. If the ceremony will be small but you have room for many guests at the reception or vice versa, be sure to tell them how many for each segment they may invite. Let them know how many announcements you will be sending out on the day of the wedding, too, and when you will need these names. You and your fiance should also list your individual friends and your mutual friends.

The Association of Bridal Consultants suggests: "The bride, her parents, the bridegroom and his parents should each compile separate lists of relatives and friends, without consulting the others. It then is up to the bride's parents to compare the lists and create the 'master list.' When the bride and bridegroom both come from the same area, the total number of guests should be divided roughly in half. On the other hand, if the bridegroom's family lives some distance away, the guest list may be weighted in favor of the bride's family, based on the reasonable expectation that fewer of the bridegroom's family can make or will be willing to make the trip." But, the Association cautions, "since it is the bride's family that hosts the reception, her family has the final word on how the guest list will be divided."

Purchase 3" x 5" cards, and divide them between your family and his family, depending on how many guests each can invite. On these little cards, you and they can write the names and addresses of the wedding guests. When they return their cards to you, file them in a card box in alphabetical order. You can check for duplications as you alphabetize the cards. Use dividers to distinguish sections for the ceremony and the reception if you are inviting different guests to each or are sending announcements. You can use these cards for keeping track of responses and wedding gifts, too. Keep this sacred box in a very safe place. Believe it or not, after twenty years I still have my box of names and addresses and use it for Christmas cards even now. Many of the guests I invited to my wedding are gone, but it is a special memento to which I have added friends' names over the years. And, don't forget to send invitations to the clergy and spouse, the bridegroom's parents, your attendants (to keep as a memento) and the parents of your attendants.

Invitations

When you look through wedding magazines and consult the stationer, you will find an array of invitation choices. For this one occasion, be traditional, even if you have a flair for the dramatic. Ultraformal and formal weddings require engraved invitations, semiformal printed, and informal calls for handwritten notes from your mother or you if you are giving the wedding yourself.

For all your wedding stationery needs, select the very highest quality paper in white if you are a Winter, off-white if you are a Summer, and creamy white if you are a Spring or Autumn. The paper will not add much to the total expense, but will reflect the importance of this occasion. You may wish to add a little color on the inside flap of the envelope for a semiformal or informal wedding only. For these less formal invitations, Winters and Summers should stay with blue or pink, Springs and Autumns with peach and aqua.

It's a good idea to select stationers that specialize in invitations and are known for the quality of their service. Shop around and ask around. Find the best. They will show you books of the various styles and paper stock, help you make your selections, and guarantee the delivery date. Basically, all you need to order are the following items:

- the invitation itself, the classic style is folded and printed on the front side

- the reception card

The most commonly used wording is...

Reception
immediately following
Columbia Country Club
12231 Connecticut Avenue
Amherst, Massachusetts

R.s.v.p.
6308 Avalon Drive
Bethesda, Maryland 20816

- an ungummed inner envelope for both the invitation and the reception card
- a larger envelope for all the enclosures.

Although you should be able to expect a handwritten reply to your invitation from every guest, it is not practical to count on it anymore. Many brides, therefore, include a response card and printed return envelope to make responding easy. These will be included inside the inner envelope, printed in the same script on the same kind of paper.

The Association of Bridal Consultants says this about response cards: "By all the canons of etiquette, a response card is incorrect and unnecessary, since the recipient of an invitation has a social obligation to send a prompt personal note of reply.... Consequently, faced with the need to provide accurate figures to caterers and other service providers, many brides have adopted the practice of enclosing 'response cards' in the hope of soliciting an early reply—or any reply at all. Studies have shown, however, that even enclosing these cards does not appreciably increase the number of responses —partly because the same social boors who can't send a personal reply also are thoughtless enough to fail to return the response card.... If response cards are used, they should be the smallest allowed by the Postal Service. A stamped, self-addressed envelope also should be provided.... One response card should be sent for each invited couple. Children and single people should receive their own."

If you are having a large wedding, pew cards may be another necessity, to be mailed after you have received a note of acceptance. These are printed invitations to sit in the ribboned-off areas of the church. For a very large wedding, all seats may be assigned. The pew cards can be printed with a blank spot for you to write in the pew number. It should read simply...

Please present this to an usher at
(name of church)
Pew No.————————————
on (date written out) Saturday the seventeenth of June

Order announcement cards to send to all those who are not invited to the wedding, but whom you wish to hear the good news. You will need just one outer envelope for the announcements. Mail them the day of, or the day after your wedding. A typical announcement would read...

Mr. and Mrs. James Arthur Brown
announce the marriage of their daughter
Celia Butler
to
Mr. Eric Forsythe Hayes
on Saturday, the seventeenth of June
Nineteen hundred and eighty-nine
at the Pilgrim Lutheran Church
Tucson, Arizona

If you have planned an ultraformal or formal wedding, you most certainly should order engraved invitations. Think of your invitation as the entrance hall to a house. It makes a very important first impression and sets the stage for the rest of your wedding.

The paper should be 100 percent cotton fiber with a kid finish, or the same watermark quality paper. The invitations can be plain or paneled. If you select the paneled style, use a shaded or block lettering style. the most popular is Shaded Antique Roman. On a plain invitation, script-style lettering is the most appropriate and, surprisingly, the least expensive. Choose from Royal Script, Florentine, Venetian, Shaded Antique Roman, Park Avenue, Stuyvesant, or Riviera, for example. Any of these will look elegant and dignified. The engraving plate will be given to you by the printer. This plate can be made into a small tray and kept as another wedding day memento.

A printing process called thermography, that fuses ink and powder to resemble engraving, is a little less expensive and can be used to look like hand-lettered Hebrew or Chinese characters. You might choose this for the engraved look, but it is really not correct for a church wedding.

Offset printed invitations are fine for the semiformal wedding ceremony if you are having more than fifty people. Otherwise, handwritten or telephoned invitations are all that is necessary for small, informal weddings.

Be sure to order extra invitations, envelopes, and enclosure cards for mistakes and memories.

Wording the Invitations

Ultraformal, formal, and semiformal invitations should read . . .

Mr. and Mrs. (your father's full name)
request the honour of your presence
at the marriage of their daughter
(your first and middle names)
to
Mr. (your fiance's full name, first, last and middle)
(day of the week) the (day of the month) of (month)
at (time spelled out)
(year written out)
name of church
street address
city, state

Every invitation contains the following information. There are some exceptions to the rule in our rapidly changing world. Here are the rules for the correctly-worded invitation which must include . . .

(1) The names of those who are extending the invitation. This is called *the invitational line* . . .

from the parents of the bride:

> Lieutenant Colonel and Mrs. Russell Burdell Warye
> Doctor and Mrs. William Jones
> Mr. and Mrs. George Miller Norris

divorced mother (use her first, maiden, and married names):

> Mrs. Edith Burton Clayton

widowed mother:

> Mrs. William Clayton

divorced parents (if your mother has not remarried):

> Mrs. Ethel Jones Brown
> Mr. Samuel Eggerton Brown

divorced parents (if your mother has remarried):

> Mrs. Gary Thomas Myers
> Mr. Samuel Eggerton Brown

if only your mother is giving the wedding:

> Mrs. Gary Thomas Myers

bride and groom:

> The honour of your presence
> is requested
> at the marriage of
> Miss Evelyn Lee Brown
> to
> Mr. Christopher Cameron Hughes

In the case of second weddings if the bride has been divorced:

The honour of your presence
is requested
at the marriage of
Mrs. Jennifer Pope Havener
to
Mr. Christopher Cameron Hughes

or

Jennifer Pope Havener
and
Christopher Cameron Hughes
request the honour of your presence
at their marriage
etc.

First names should be written in full, no nicknames, please. Don't abbreviate titles except for Mr. and Mrs. Doctor and Junior should be spelled out. If you're marrying a III or IV, be certain the typeface you choose can handle it. One bride had not anticipated this quirk in typefaces and rather than use an awkward succession of capital I's, we found a calligrapher to duplicate the flow of the script before the invitations went off to be printed. Sounds relatively simple, but it could have cost the bride a lot of extra money.

(2) *The request line* which extends the invitation...

for a house of worship:

request the honour of your presence
at the marriage of their daughter

for a wedding at home or at a club:

request the pleasure of your company
at the marriage of their daughter

Note spelling of the word *honour.* It is spelled with a *u* on wedding invitations, just as it has been in England for centuries. The word *favour* also has a *u* on formal invitations.

(3). *The bride's name,* note the exceptions described previously...
Ordinarily only the bride's given names are used:

Sara Clayton

However, if your mother has remarried and has a different last name from the bride, the bride's full name should be given:

Sara Clayton Hughes

Do not precede the bride's name with "Miss."

(4) *The joining clauses.* This is the little article that links your name to his. Use "to" except on invitation to a marriage reception in which case "and" would be used

(5) *The groom's name...*
Full name preceded by title (Mr., Doctor)
Do not use initials

Doctor Daniel Lephart Grant
Captain William Asbury Schaefer
Mr. Elliot Richardson Green

(6) *The date line...*

Saturday, the tenth of May

(7) *The year line.* Write it out in words, not numbers. Actually, the year line is not necessary, though not incorrect, on an invitation; but must always be used on an announcement...

One thousand, nine hundred and eighty-nine
or
Nineteen hundred and eighty-nine

(8) *The time of the ceremony...*

at four o'clock
at half after four o'clock

The time of the ceremony is always written out, "at four o'clock" or "at half after four o'clock." Quarter hours are not used, nor do you say, "a.m." or "p.m." You can add "in the morning" or "in the evening" if you think there might be some confusion, particularly when the ceremony will take place at eight or nine o'clock. When the wedding is at noon, the hour may be designated as "at high noon" or "at twelve o'clock" or "at twelve o'clock noon." If the wedding is during daylight savings time, say "daylight savings time" so that out-of-town guests will arrive on time.

(9) *Name of church* in full... "Saint" is always spelled out.

The Church of the Redeemer
Saint Patrick's Cathedral
The Washington Hebrew Congregation

(10) *Address of church.* This is not necessary unless there are two churches with the same name in the same locality.

4201 Dunrobbin Drive
Fifth Avenue
8511 Macomb Street, Northwest

(11) *City and state...*

Cincinnati, Ohio

There are two exceptions to this rule:

New York
City of Washington

(12) *Corner lines.* If the ceremony and reception are at the same location, reply request lines are shown in lower left corner...

The favour of a reply is requested
307 West Shore Road
Huntington, New York 11743

Black tie - Not proper but can be shown in lower right hand corner. Never use "Black tie preferred."*Breakfast* is the word used for the celebration after the ceremony, if it is before one o'clock in the afternoon, *reception* after one.

When the reception is being held at the same place as the ceremony, include the phrase "Reception at six o'clock" in the lower left hand corner. "R.s.v.p." or "Please reply to" with the address of the appropriate parent should also appear in the lower left hand corner.

A formal Roman Catholic ceremony may have a little different wording in the invitation...

Mr. and Mrs. Brian Houlihan
request the honour of your presence
at the Nuptial Mass uniting their daughter
Mary Louise
and
Mr. Patrick Sean O'Casey
in the Sacrament of Holy Matrimony
etc.

Notice that Mary Louise and Patrick are being united and the word *and* is used instead of *to.*

A Jewish wedding at a hotel or club should read...

Mr. and Mrs. Herbert Gold
request the pleasure of your company
at the marriage of their daughter
Elizabeth Ann
to
Mr. Charles Levin
son of
Mr. and Mrs. Louis Morris Levin
on Wednesday, the fifth of June
One thousand nine hundred and eighty-nine
at half after three o'clock
Hotel Washington
Miami, Florida
Reception at five o'clock

When the wedding is to take place at a synagogue, say...

Mr. and Mrs. Herbert Gold
Mr. and Mrs. Louis Morris Levin
request the honour of your presence
at the marriage of their children
Elizabeth Ann
and
Mr. Charles Levin
Wednesday, the fifth of June
One thousand nine hundred and eighty-nine
at half after three o'clock
Congregation Ahev Shalom
Miami

Notice that the names of both sets of parents are included, the word
and is used instead of *to,* and *children* is used instead of daughter.

When the reception is not being held at the same place, the reception
card is very simple. It can read . . .

Reception
immediately following the ceremony
The Columbia Country Club

The favour of a reply is requested
6308 Avalon Drive
Bethesda, Maryland 20816

If you are having a limited number of people to the wedding ceremony, but are having a large reception, you may say...

Mr. and Mrs. Albert Finney
request the pleasure of your company
at the marriage reception of their daughter
Melissa Jane
to
Mr. Herbert Burford Bulle
on Saturday, the seventeenth of June
at five o'clock
The Saint Regis Hotel
New York

The favour of a reply is requested:
5702 Newburn Drive
New Canaan, Connecticut 06840

Note the time given is one hour after that set for the ceremony. To those invited to both the ceremony and the reception, enclose a small card of invitation which says...

Ceremony
at four o'clock
Saint Paul's Cathedral

If everyone is to be invited to the ceremony and the reception, you may word the invitation...

Mr. and Mrs. Egbert Miller
request the honour of your presence
at the marriage of their daughter
Eloise Ann
to
Mr. John Baker Smith
on Saturday, the seventeenth of June
at four o'clock
Saint Paul's Cathedral
and afterwards at the reception
The Saint Regis Hotel
New York

R.s.v.p.
5902 Ramsgate Road
Honolulu, Hawaii 98654

Addressing the Invitations

Now comes the fun. All invitations and announcements must be addressed by hand. Call in all responsible members of your family with good handwriting and get to work. The inner envelopes may arrive already stuffed with the invitation and enclosure cards. It is no longer necessary to leave in the tissues that have been inserted by the printer to protect the invitations from ink smears. Check each one to make sure the reception card and any other inserts are included inside the ungummed envelopes. The outer envelopes will be in separate boxes, so they can be addressed and then filled with the appropriate invitation materials. You can usually get the outside envelopes before the engraved materials, and begin addressing, unless you are having your return address printed on the outside. If you are using an embosser to put on your return address, addressing can begin ahead of time. For an ultraformal wedding, you may want to hire a calligrapher to do the addressing. All the invitations will look elegant and formal.

On the outside of the inner envelope simply write the title and last names of the guests, for example, Mr. and Mrs. Jones or Ms. Freeman. Children can either be addressed as "Miss" or "Master" and their name or simply by their first names if several are included in the invitation. Address intimate relatives by the names you call them, for instance, "Aunt Bess."

Address the outside envelope with the title and full names of the guests and their addresses. Titles, such as General, Senator, The Reverend, should not be abbreviated. Names should be written out in full—first, middle, and last names. Do not use abbreviations except for the standard Mr. and Mrs. Streets, cities, and states should be written in full with zip codes.

Mailing the Invitations

Before you apply the postage, have one invitation weighed at the post office and purchase the correct stamp or stamps. Order an embosser and use it for your return address or have your printer do this for you. Formal invitations must be mailed at least four weeks in advance. Keep in mind that out-of-town guests may need thirty days for air fare arrangements and you want to be considerate, so try to get their invitations out in plenty of time. Handwritten invitations may be mailed two or three weeks in advance.

At-Home Cards

Many couples have at-home cards printed to go with their announcements. These cards simply state your new address. Typical wording is...

At Home
after the first of August
6502 Brett Lane
San Francisco, California 98742

The Association of Bridal Consultants notes: "The traditional form is flawed, since many recipients may neglect to note the name on the card or enter the address immediately in an address book. Therefore, it is becoming acceptable to include the couple's married name. This also is an acceptable way of noting that the bride will retain her maiden name or that the couple will combine surnames." The Association offers these two examples of the modern approach. Wording such as the following may be included on the at-home card with your new address:

Planning the Ceremony

Janis Johnson
will retain her surname
after her marriage to
William J. Faye
Your cooperation in this regard is appreciated

Jeannie and Tom
after marriage
will share the surname
Cross-Woodman
Your cooperation in this regard
is appreciated

The Wedding at Home

If your wedding is to take place at home with a small intimate group of friends and family, handwritten notes should go out inviting your guests. A sample of such a note is...

Dear Kathleen (no punctuation)

Sara and William Bradley are being married at the Church of the Redeemer on Saturday, March the twelfth at three o'clock. We hope you and Neil will be able to come to the ceremony, and afterward to our home.

Affectionately,

Lauren Smith

Time for Thanks

The perfect time to order fine quality plain or engraved notepaper for writing your thank-you notes is when you order your invitations. Every note must be handwritten by the bride, who is the traditional recipient of all the gifts, as soon after the arrival of each gift as possible.

The classic thank you note should be written in blue or black ink on fine, folded note paper similar to that of your invitations. You may want to have your new name engraved on the front. Of course, you won't be able to mail your thank-you notes until after the wedding when your new name will be officially yours, but you will be able to use the stationery for your new life, not just your engagement. Decide now when you will have more time for writing to thank people for their thoughtfulness, before or after the ceremony, and how you may use these engraved informals in the future as party invitations, thank you notes, and so forth.

Mention the gift by name and how you plan to use it in your new life. Be warm and gracious; thank-you notes leave long-lasting impressions. Sign your first name only to intimate friends, your full name to newer acquaintances and older friends of the family. Emboss or hand write your return address on the back of the envelope. Saying thank you is one of your most important jobs. We recommend doing it as quickly and graciously as you can.

Changes in Plans

Sometimes tragedies or changed-minds can affect your wedding plans. If you must cancel your wedding after the invitations have been sent, you must notify your guests immediately. Last-minute cancellations require telegrams and telephone calls. If you have time, you may send printed notification. The Association of Bridal Consultants offer these examples:

Mr. and Mrs. Jerrold Norman Finnie
regret that owing to a death in the family
the invitations to
their daughter's wedding
on Saturday, February seventh
must be recalled

Owing to the death of
Mrs. Charles Fischbein
the marriage of her daughter
Felicia
to
Mr. Jerry Alan Green
has been postponed.

Signing Contracts

We'll discuss the florist and the musicians in the next chapter, but don't forget to begin your search for a photographer. The photographer will be in charge of taking those official pictures of the bride and the bridal party before the ceremony, during the ceremony, and at the reception. Be sure his or her contract includes all of the services you expect: how many photos to be taken, how long you can keep the proofs before deciding which photos you want, whether or not you will receive an album, the time that will be spent taking the photographs and where (in your home before the ceremony, in the house of worship or club, at the reception).

Use the checklist in Chapter 3 to make sure you have covered all the points when you discuss each service with the appropriate vendor.

Chapter 8
Coloring the Ceremony

Your Personal Touches

Now that you have the basics set and the invitations ordered, it's time to think about the colorful parts of the ceremony—the flowers and the music. These are personal touches you will add to the traditions. Be sure you check with your clergy or the management at the place of your ceremony to find out what restrictions there may be. In some churches, the altar guild does the flowers for the altar. In others, music is strictly prescribed.

Here is a list of things to find out about your chosen place of worship or ceremony site. Ask...

1. What is the seating capacity?

2. What fee is expected for the clergy, organist, and sexton?

3. Are people to light the candles available?

4. Can flash photographs be taken in the church? Can any photographs be taken in the church during the ceremony and/or during the rehearsal?

5. Is there an aisle runner?

6. Does the church provide candles, candelabra, kneeling pillows for the bride and groom?

7. Are there restrictions on where flower arrangements and candelabra can be placed?

8. May you reserve time for the rehearsal at the place of worship?

Ask now while you still have time to make alternate arrangements.

Flowers

You have made your tour of the church, synagogue, or other facility where the ceremony will take place. You've noted the formality, decor, and mood of the setting. Winters, your ideal wedding would take place in a rather stylized formal space with dark woods, painted or lacquered moldings and seats, shiny or silky fabrics, silver-tone metals, clear cool colors. Summers, your space should be stately and traditional with light-to-medium woods, painted or antiqued moldings and seats, floral patterns, fabrics with a soft sheen, silver-toned or rose-gold metals. Autumns will look best in a space with medium-to-dark woods and antiqued moldings and seats, textured fabrics, and antique brass. Springs, surround yourself with light-to-medium woods, fabrics with a bright sheen, polished brass, and clear warm colors. However, if the setting you have chosen does not meet these stylistic characteristics, you can "redecorate" it with flowers.

Flowers are the symbol of love and will link the colors in your palette to the setting of the ceremony. Of course, you and your attendants and guests will color the ceremony with your clothes and accessories. But the true link will be the flowers. They should blend the setting with the wedding party and set the mood.

You will be purchasing flowers for your own bouquet and perhaps for your headpiece, bouquets for your attendants, boutonnieres for the groomsmen and your father or the man who will take you down the aisle, and your groom's father—traditionally, these are paid for by the groom—corsages for your mother and your groom's mother and other special aunts and grandmothers, and floral arrangements for the church and reception. That's a big job and a major expense. If you have retained a wedding consultant, she will help you locate the best florist and work with you and the floral designer to achieve the best floral effects. If you are on your own, take your color palette and your ideas on an interviewing tour of florists in town. Ask friends and relatives for recommendations. But meet personally with different florists to see if you like their ideas and prices. If you can, start at least six months ahead of time in this important quest. Your florist can provide aisle ribbons, the aisle carpet, and sometimes the ring pillow. Some churches have this equipment, including altar vases, candelabras, and standing vases which your florist and you should inspect and use.

Flowers are the ultimate accessory. Not only are you looking for the colors that will enhance you and your wedding, you are also searching for the kinds of flowers and arrangements that reflect your personal style and the mood of the event. Flowers can be dramatic, classic, romantic, or absolutely free and natural. If you are having an ultraformal wedding, go with the dramatic. If you've chosen to be formal, choose dignified, traditional arrangements. The semiformal wedding will be complemented by romantic allusions. And, the informal wedding should be accentuated by natural-looking arrangements with flowers native to your region.

Flowers for Winters are the most dramatic in nature's repertoire. Decorate your wedding with long-stemmed roses or sculptured lilies, hothouse azaleas and poinsettia plants. Flowers for Summers come right off your palette: irises in your cool blues and roses and gladiolas in your flattering pinks. Autumn's flowers bloom in your season: mums, marigolds, asters, and zinnias; yellow daisies, strawflowers, and wheat for a country room reception. And, Spring, your flowers are so lovely they were made for weddings: lilies-of-the-valley, baby's breath, carnations, narcissus, sweetheart roses, and violets; daisies for a simple garden or at-home ceremony. Of course, you must consider the time of year and time of day your wedding will take place. Choosing flowers that are out of season can be more costly and may be impossible to obtain. This is a perfect reason to set the date in your own season.

Bouquets

Bouquets can be crescent-shaped, cascading, set on a prayer book, or grouped in a romantic nosegay. Roman brides carried herbs in bunches. Orange blossoms, orchids, gardenias, stephanotis, carnations, and roses are popular bouquet favorites today. Your florist can add imagination to your list of flowers and come up with a creation that reflects your personal style as well as your palette of colors.

The bouquet should be in proportion to your height and follow the line of your dress. The color and variety will depend on *your* season, the time of year, and the degree of formality. Give your florist a complete description of your dress including a sketch or photograph and a fabric swatch if available.

Flowers that simulate the texture of the fabric help to relate the dress to the flowers and pull the entire look together. If your dress is of romantic silk organza, marquisette, or tulle, your flowers should carry out that airy, cloudlike illusion, too. A bouquet of sweetheart roses, stephanotis, and lilies-of-the-valley or violets bunched with tulle and ribbon will repeat the look of the romantic, filmy and ruffled gown.

A dramatic satin gown would be perfect with a bouquet of orchids, stephanotis, and garlands of white pearls, while a more classic gown in softer peau de soie will be enhanced by a bouquet of gardenias, roses, and stephanotis.

Camellias with their natural foliage or a romantic rose bouquet will be just right for your Victorian gown of taffeta and lace. If you are wearing a simple lace mantilla, consider carrying a lace fan decorated with a few camellias or gardenias. A fur muff with a single poinsettia will complement your white velvet dress for a Christmas wedding. White daisies, carnations, and bachelor buttons in baskets are perfect with cotton eyelet or dotted swiss for a country wedding. A parasol of the same fabric would be a charming accessory with an antebellum-style dress. For that "something blue," ask your florist about adding a tiny cluster of blue forget-me-nots or other blue flowers behind your bouquet.

An important consideration in selecting flowers for your bouquet is their life expectancy. It is important that the flowers look fresh until the very end of the reception. Most orchids, roses, carnations, stephanotis, chrysanthemums, and majestic daisies last longer while gardenias, camelias, violets, long-stemmed roses, and phalaenopsis orchids have a shorter life expectancy.

To give a feeling of continuity to the procession, the bride's and bridesmaids' bouquets should be similar in design and color. If your bridesmaids' dresses are not all the same color, the bouquets should include all the colors. If their dresses match, their bouquets should match. For a dignified but smashing look, have each bouquet a shade lighter or darker in the same color as the dress of the attendant. A junior bridesmaid should carry the same type of bouquet as the bridesmaids, scaled down in proportion to suit her size.

Decorating the Ceremony

Church or Synagogue Weddings. Large floral arrangements in urns, trees in pots, baskets of country flowers, flower-decked arches, a luxurious canopy over the Jewish bridal couple are all designs you and your florist can

Coloring the Ceremony

create for your ceremony. Decorating the pews, doors, and balustrades with delicate garlands of leaves and flowers or big ribbon bows. An evening wedding with tall candelabras and silver ribbons creates a dramatic Winter ceremony.

Floral arrangements for the church should be planned to complement its architecture and size. Large churches with dramatic architectural flourishes need arrangements that not only have form but shape and mass. If your florist is not familiar with the church, take him or her there for an advance tour. The lighting effects—whether sunlight or artificial—and spotlights should also be studied carefully. The time of day and year may affect the amount of sunlight streaming in.

Try to use flowers that are in season. The wise Winter who is marrying during the Christmas season can take advantage of the church's own festive decorations of wreaths, red and white ribbons, and greens. Add your own small Christmas trees lighted by tiny candles (be careful!) or tiny white lights and bank them on the altar with potted poinsettias. If you have planned an all-white or "snowball" wedding, red roses or red carnations can be combined with Christmas trees and your attendants can carry them too. On the other hand, if you are a Winter marrying in the springtime, use potted tulips or white lilies, lush and lovely in those months.

The prudent Summer who is planning a June wedding, can decorate the altar with white roses and lilacs. Later in the summer, she has long spikes of gladioli, available from July to September, to create the classic calm she loves. The long stems will be visible from quite a distance in a large church. The shorter spikes can be used for aisle decorations with candelabra. Delphiniums are another choice for Summers and come in tall and short stems.

The clever Autumn who plans a fall wedding, has many large colorful flowers to choose from. Combine giant dahlias, zinnias, or chrysanthemums with autumn leaves on the altar and with zinnias down the aisles.

And that bright Spring who is having an April wedding can fill her church with hybrid white or yellow forsythia and daffodils, lilies of-the-valley, even cherry and apple blossoms.

The center aisle of the church should have candles, floral arrangements on tall stands, or lovely white satin ribbons tied in large bows on some or all of the pews. An aisle carpet should be used at an ultraformal or formal wedding. Aisle carpets are from 30 to 36 inches wide and should stretch from the altar down the aisle to the back pews with about six feet to spare. The extra six feet will allow your train to be adjusted before you come into view of the guests. The kneeling bench, or prie-dieu, in front of the altar is an addition you and your groom will appreciate. It can be decorated with white pillows for the kneeling level.

Home, Hotel, or Club Wedding. Even more careful planning and attention to detail is necessary to create the lovely setting you want for the ceremony without the religious trappings of a house of worship. You will need to develop your own "altar" or focal point for the actual ceremony.

In most homes—whether private or a club setting—the best place for the ceremony is in the living room in front of the fireplace. If the lines of the fireplace are right, you may only need two arrangements of flowers, placed as close as possible to each end of the mantel with candles behind them. Or, you could use a pair of ivy trees lavishly adorned with flowers, or for a Christmas wedding, miniature Christmas trees.

If there is no fireplace, a large window can provide an ideal background, or place urns of flowers or potted trees in a mass around a special rug to set your stage.

If you are fortunate enough to have a circular staircase, it can be decorated with white satin ribbons, greenery and flowers. Suggest an aisle for you to walk down by lining a path between the chairs to the fireplace with the same flowers, ribbons, and greenery.

Outside in the garden, who cares whether you have a fireplace or a circular staircase? You have the sky, trees, and all of nature. But you do need to create a setting for the ceremony. Large urns of field flowers set on pedestals, potted trees, a canopy or floral arch, votive candles or potted plants lining the path to the clergymember can create the same illusion outside as in. Make sure you select a spot where the guests can see what is going on. And, just in case it might rain, consider renting a tent. A wonderful place to be married is a colorful striped tent dancing on the lawn. Decorate the tables with flowers and candles for the reception.

Boutonnieres for the Men in Your Life

The groom pays for the boutonnieres for his attendants and both fathers, but you can help him choose them so that they will blend with the other flowers. Suggest that your florist handle these for him; it makes everything much simpler.

For any type of ceremony, lilies-of-the-valley, stephanotis, or white carnations are appropriate for the groom. For more formal ceremonies, the other men in the wedding party should wear gardenias or white carnations. For less formal weddings, the best man, ushers, and the fathers should wear white carnations or carnations tinted to match the bridesmaids' flowers. If the groom is wearing a white coat, a maroon carnation makes a vivid contrast.

Flowers for Every Season

Winter	Summer	Autumn	Spring
Roses	Roses	Asters	Roses
Lilies	Carnations	Marigolds	Carnations
Tulips	Gladiolas	Chrysanthemums	Violets
Carnations	Sweet peas	Zinnias	Baby's breath
Camellias	Gardenias	Begonias (red)	Lilies-of-the
Poinsettias	Jasmine	Mimosas	-valley
Orchids	Orange-	Stock	Narcissus
Violets	blossoms		Daisies
	Begonias (pink)		
	Lilacs		
	Stephanotis		

Music—Color for Ears

Music is another mood-setting element of your wedding ceremony. Religious selections are appropriate for church or temple weddings. Discuss your musical preferences with your clergy and the music director. They will guide you in choices that are appropriate for the occasion and can recommend musicians or singers to perform during the service. The organ is the most common instrument, but it can be enriched with a harp, flute, brass instruments (particularly for your triumphant march down the aisle), even a string quartet.

If you'd like a soloist, a quartet, or the church choir, you must check with the organist before you make your final selections. Many churches have a requirement that all wedding music, vocal or instrumental, be approved by the choir director. This music should take place after most of the guests have been seated but before the ceremony begins. Time the last song to take place just before the wedding march, while the mothers are being escorted by the ushers to their seats. It's a good idea to have the vocalist go through this part of the program at your rehearsal so that everyone will know when to begin.

Traditionally, a soft prelude begins about half an hour before the service while your guests are being seated. Rousing classics like Mozart's "The Marriage of Figaro" will introduce dramatic Winter brides with a flourish. Stately classics like Debussy's "Claire de Lune" reflect Summer's flavor. Springs might choose a Mozart classic for that clear, fresh feel. Autumns, how about "Horn Pipe" from *Water Music* by Handel?

Then you must think about your entrance...What sort of music will reflect you? Listen to music in the months before your wedding. Jot down the names of pieces that impress you. Then talk to your clergy or the music director about them.

Popular choices are the "Bridal Chorus" from Wagner's *Lohengrin* and the "Wedding March" from Mendelssohn's *Midsummer Night's Dream;* Tchaikovsy's "Apeothesis" from *Sleeping Beauty;* Williams' "Doxology;" the "Prince of Denmark's March" by Clarke, Cuperin's "Fanfare" from *The Triumphant;* and Handel's "Sarabande" from *Suite No. 11* are selections you should listen to and consider for that most important march.

You may want to have soft music during the ceremony as well. A hymn or other religious favorite that is meaningful to both of you is always appropriate.

And don't forget the march out. The recessional is usually preceded by organ chimes or the ringing of carillon bells just before the march begins. Your recessional should be a triumph too. Try Knecht's "Psalm 100," Mouret's "Rondo," or Buxtehude's "Fugue in C Minor."

To give you some idea of the flow of music, here is a program for the formal wedding as suggested by Dr. Eileen Morris Guenther, a member of the music faculty of The George Washington University and Minister of Music at Foundry United Methodist Church in Washington, D.C. Dr. Guenther produces a weekly program on organ music, "The Royal Instrument," on WGMS AM/FM. Here is her very extensive list from which you can make your selections. If you want to hear any of them ahead of time, write to Dr. Guenther at WGMS, 11300 Rockville Pike, Rockville, MD 20852. She can supply you with recording numbers which you can take to your local record store.

Organ Music for the Wedding Prelude

Composer	Title
Alain	Postlude for the Office of Compline
Bach	Bist du bei mir
Bach	Jesu, Joy of Man's Desiring
Bach	Deck thyself, my soul, with Gladness
Bach	Wake, awake
Brahms	Deck thyself, my soul, with Gladness
Bridge	Adagio in E
Buxtehude	"Gigue" Fugue
Buxtehude	Prelude, Fuge and Chaconne
Campra	Rigaudon
Cook	Fanfare
Couperin	Chaconne in G Minor
Davis, Henry Walford	Solemn Melody
Dubois	Toccata in G
Dupre	Cortege and Litany
Dupre	Musette
Elgar	"Nimrod" from Enigma Variations (arr. Harris)
Gigout	Scherzo in E Major
Gigout	Toccata in B Minor
Greene	Voluntary in C
Handel	Air from "Water Music"
Haydn	Flute clock pieces
Langlais	selections from Neuf Pieces
Marcello	Psalm 19
Mathias	Processional
Peeters	Aria
Preston	Alleluyas
Purcell	Voluntary on "The Old Hundredth"
Stanley	Voluntary in C
Vaughan Williams	Three Preludes on Welsh Hymn Tunes
Vierne	Impromptu from "Pieces de Fantaisie, Suite 3"
Wesley	Choral Song and Fugue
Wright	Prelude on Broth James's Air

In addition to these pieces there is a large recital repertory that may provide a good deal of appropriate music for the wedding prelude. For instance, an organist may wish to include:

- German baroque Preludes and Fuges or Chorale Preludes by Bach, Bohm, Buxtehude, Pachelbel, Scheidt, Schroeder, Telemann, Walther; French Classical pieces by Clerambault, Couperin, Dandrieu, Daquin, DuMage, Grigny, Guilain, LeBegue;

- 18th-Century English Voluntaries by Boyce, Grene, Bennett, Stanley, Wesley;

- French Romantic pieces by Franck, Widor, Vierne, Tournemire, Guilmant, Gigout;

- German Romantic pieces by Mendelssohn, Schumann, Liszt, Rheinberger, Reger, Karg-Elert;

- 20th-Century preludes on hymn tunes by Bender, Near, Peeters, Pepping, Rohlig, Willan.

Organ Processionals and Recessionals

Composer	Title
Bach	Toccata in F
Campra	Rigaudon
Clarke	Prince of Denmark's March
Coke-Jephcott	Bishop's Promenade
Elgar	Imperial March
Franck	Piece-Heroique
Gigout	Grand Choeur Dialogue
Guilmant	March Religieuse
Handel	Fanfare from "Water Music"
Jackson	Archbishop's Fanfare
Karg-Elert	March Triomphale
Lang	Fanfare
Lang	Tuba Tune
Leighton	Paean
Marcello	Psalm 19

Composer	Title
Mathias	Processional
Mouret	Rondeau
Mulet	Tu es Petrus
Purcell	Selections of trumpet tunes
Stanley	Trumpet Voluntary and Tune in D
Vierne	Carillon de Westminster
Vierne	Final, Symphony I
Vierne	Marche Episcopale
Walton	Crown Imperial March
Widor	Toccata, Symphony V
Wills	Fanfare in D

Music for Organ and Instruments

These are just a few of the musical selections available for a combination of organ and other instruments (equally suitable, in many cases, for the Wedding Prelude or as a Processional or Recessional).

Composer	Title
Organ and Trumpet	
Clarke	Prince of Denmark's March
Mouret	Sinfonies de Fanfares
Purcell	Ceremonial Music
Purcell	Trumpet Tune
Stanley	Voluntary in D
Telemann	Heldenmusik
Torelli	Concerto in D
Torelli	Sinfonia
Vivaldi	Sonata Prima
Organ and Two Trumpets	
Bach	My Spirit be Joyful
Manfredini	Concert in D

**Organ, Brass
and Percussion**

Bliss	Ceremonial Prelude
Dupre	Poeme Heroique
Widor	Lord, Save thy People

Organ and Violin

Holler	Fantasie for Violin and Organ, Op. 49
Kaminski	Canzona
Rheinberger	Suite for Violin and Organ, Op. 166

Organ and Cello

Holler	Improvisation on "Schonster Herr. Jesu," Op. 55
Kirchner	Two Pieces, Op. 92
Saint-Saens	Priere

Organ and Strings

Albrechtsberger	Concerto in B-flat
Graun	Concerto in F
Handel	16 Organ Concerti
Haydn, J.	Concerto in C
Haydn, M.	Concerto in C
Mozart	Church Sonatas
Stanley	Concerto #5 in A

**Organ and
Flute or Recorder**

Handel	Sonata in F, Op. 1, #11
Marcello	Sonata in G
Martin	Sonata da Chiesa
Telemann	Partita #2 in G

**Organ and Oboe
or English Horn**

Hertel	Partitas I and II
Koetsier	Partita for English Horn and Organ
Krebs	Fantaisie in F Minor for Oboe and Organ

(Reprinted with permission of Eileen Morris Guenther.)

The Cokesbury Marriage Manual suggests this program for a home wedding if you are having an electric organ, a string organ, a string trio, a harp and trio, or a harp and violin...

Spring Song by Mendelsohn
Toujours L'Amour by Friml
Dreams by Schumann
Aria of Nicolante from Lake for Cello
Song of Songs by Rimsky-Korsokov
March by Svendson

And now let's practice...

Chapter 9
Rehearsals and Other Parties

All the World's a Stage

Every great drama requires rehearsal. A wedding usually only gets one. Traditionally, it is scheduled for the afternoon or early evening before the actual ceremony. Some believe it should be held two or three days before the ceremony, so that the rehearsal dinner held afterwards can be a real party. It's a good idea to save the night before the wedding for sleep. But if your attendants—or you and your groom, for that matter—can only get to town the day before the wedding, set the rehearsal for early evening, about 5:30, and the dinner right afterward.

The Players

All of your attendants and your bridegroom's, both sets of parents, the organist and any other scheduled musicians and singers, your clergymember, and you and your groom should all be there ready to perfect your parts for the wedding ceremony. Invite everyone by phone or postcard, and make sure they are prompt. Dress up. Jeans and slacks just don't create the mood you want for this important occasion. All the players need to be alert and responsive.

Your clergymember is the director. This is his show and only he or she can give directions on how the ceremony will be conducted. Basically, there are three parts to the modern wedding ceremony: the betrothal, exchange of vows, and benediction. But first you must march in.

You can practice with a bouquet made up of the ribbons from the presents you received at your bridal shower. If your church permits and if you will be wearing a train, you may also want to tie a sheet around your waist to get the feel of walking with a long train.

The Processional

As the wedding processional begins, the clergy, groom, and best man come in from the vestry or right-hand side of the room. The clergy stands facing the congregation, with the groom at his right, and the best man just behind him.

Then in march the ushers, leading the procession, and marching in pairs. Try to match the men in each pair by height. At the end of the aisle, they separate, and go to stand on either the left or right hand side of the hall, near the front and facing the altar.

Behind the ushers come your pretty bridesmaids in pairs. Or if you have an uneven number, they should march one behind the other, about six feet apart. The maid of honor always marches alone about eight feet behind the last bridesmaids. At the end of the aisle the bridesmaids separate, just as the ushers did, and stand in front of the ushers on each side. The maid of honor at the head of the line, where she can help the bride.

After the maid of honor come your ring bearer and flower girl. And, then here comes the bride. . .

If you are a Jewish bride a few more people will have preceded you. Awaiting you at the altar will be the cantor and rabbi. Leading the procession will be your grandparents, followed by your groom's grandparents, then his ushers and best man. Behind him comes your dear groom flanked by his parents, then your bridesmaids and maid of honor, and last comes you, the blushing bride, flanked by your parents. . .

You will march in leaning on the right arm of your father or another honored male relative. When you reach the end of the aisle, you and your father will stop and your groom will walk to your right side, and you will step two steps forward together in front of the clergy. Your father will remain standing where he is until the clergyman asks, "Who gives this woman to be married?" He will answer, "Her mother and I do," take your right hand and put it into the clergyman's hand, then return to his seat next to your mother. And the marriage proceeds according to the traditions of your religion or the service you have prepared.

Rehearsals and Other Parties

Your parents will remain standing at the altar with you, but ouside the canopy, in a Jewish ceremony. When the service is over, you and your groom march out first, followed by your parents, then his, then your maid of honor and bridesmaids, the ushers and best man, and the rabbi.

If you are being married at home, and you do not have a staircase to descend, the wedding party should practice assembling outside the entrance to the living room and taking their cue from the music to begin the procession. After you have been pronounced man and wife, in a home, there is no recessional. Simply turn around and greet your guests. Then the celebration can begin.

Processional

Traditional Jewish   **Christian**

During the Service

Christian

Traditional Jewish

1. Bride 2. Groom 3. Maid of Honor
4. Best Man 5. Bridesmaids
6. Ushers 7. Flower Girl 8. Ring
Bearer 9. Father of the Bride
10. Mother of the Bride
11. Father of the Groom

12. Mother of the Groom
13. Clergymember
14. Cantor 15. Bride's Grandfather
16. Bride's Grandmother
17. Groom's Grandfather
18. Groom's Grandmother

The Recessional

After the Christian service, the bride takes her bouquet from her maid of honor, takes the groom's right arm and you march together back down the aisle, smiling and greeting guests along the way. Your attendants follow in reverse order, escorted by an usher if there are an equal number of them, the maid of honor escorted by the best man, of course.

The flower girl, ring bearer, and junior bridesmaids should follow right after the bride and groom. Sometimes the little people simply march out hand-in-hand with their parents.

All of this you will practice at the rehearsal. The organist should play the music you have chosen together, so that everyone in the party knows their cues. Everyone should begin the march with their left foot and walk about four pews behind the person in front. Your bridesmaids should be instructed in the graceful slow walk in time to the music or the more dramatic hesitation step which is harder to maintain in perfect unison.

Don't overrehearse the ring bearer and flower girl. These little friends can get nervous or bored—or both—if they have to do too much before the ceremony. They might refuse to participate when you really want them.

Exceptions to the Rule

The Double Wedding. Okay, Doublemint Twins, be ready for double the pleasure and double the fun, but also double the complexity for this wedding with two brides and two grooms. Of course, you will have harmonized all the colors and costumes, but who actually goes first down the aisle? Traditionally, it is the older bride. But sometimes a father will escort one sister on each arm down to the altar. If you are friends, not sisters, you each have a father as escort. Be sure you select a church or hall with plenty of room for two wedding parties and attendants, although you may be maid and matron of honor to each other.

The Military Wedding. Here is the wedding of Pomp and Circumstance, complete with shining swords and uniforms. Certainly the military wedding calls for your groom to be in the armed services, his ushers are all fellow military friends (although the best man can be a civilian), and for both of you to want an ultraformal or formal ceremony. If you live with your parents on a base, you may choose the chaplain to officiate, in which case all garrison officers and their wives should be invited to the wedding and the reception. If your wedding is not on the base, your groom's post commander and commanding officer with their spouses should be included.

The bride and groom stand under the national and regimental colors or unit standards. White flowers are appropriate for the altar and aisle-post decorations. Flags may be crossed or stand alone. The procession is similar to the civilian ceremony, but the recession is where "sparks fly," if the groom is a commissioned officer. The ushers draw their swords on command and the bride and groom pass under the arch, followed by the maid of honor and best man, then the bridesmaids, two by two. The ushers go out the side door, rush to the chapel steps and form the arch again for the bridal party to pass through. Another way is for the ushers to escort the bridesmaids in the recessional after the bride and groom have passed under the arch for the first time. The ushers' left hands must be left free to carry their caps, held with visor pointing left oblique.

Military rank dictates who sits where at a sit-down reception. Dress uniforms should be worn for very formal peacetime weddings, regulation uniforms for wartime. All members of the military should leave their caps in the vestibule but may wear side arms. Boutonnieres are not worn with uniforms.

Decisions, Decisions . . .

The rehearsal is the time to decide whether your maid or matron of honor will hold your bouquet during the ceremony, who will hold the groom's ring in a double ring ceremony, whether you want your attendant or the groom to hold back your veil at the altar, when the soloist should sing (before the wedding march at a shorter ceremony and during the ceremony at a nuptual mass), and many other matters that will come up during this important rehearsal time.

Those chosen to light the candles should have instructions. If no acolytes or special candle lighters are available, lighting the candles will become part of the ushers' jobs. The altar candles are lighted first. Then the candelabra on either side, starting at the center and moving toward the outside candles. The aisle candles should be lighted last. Candle lighting can be a lovely part of the ceremony as the candle lighters slowly light up the church or synagogue. Candle lighters, watch each other and try to keep their movements in unison. It will add to the ceremony.

Plan with the ushers how you want the church emptied. Should the ushers "bow out" each row, or the guests follow after your parents and the groom's parents exit.

Instructions for the Ushers

While the bridesmaids are learning the wedding march, your ushers should be learning exactly how they will perform their duties, including the escorting of the guests to their seats. Now is the time to remind them that about five minutes before the ceremony begins, one of them will escort your groom's mother to her seat into the right-hand front pew. The bridegroom's father follows a few steps behind her. Your mother will be escorted to her seat in the left-hand front pew right before the ceremony is to begin. She is the last person to be seated and her arrival is the signal that the service is about to start.

Two ushers then walk to the front of the church, lifting the front pew ribbons and pulling them over the tops of the pews down to the back of the church. They may also put down the aisle canvas along the aisle. The florist will have left it folded accordion fashion at the back of the church so that it can be pulled easily down the aisle.

If you are having a large ultraformal wedding, you may want to make their job easier by giving each usher a typed list of guests with who sits where. Pew cards giving each guest an assigned seat are also appropriate for large weddings.

The usher asks the guests' name at the door, asks him or her on which side they would like to sit if there are neither pew cards nor a formal list, then escorts them to the proper seat. Guests should wait at the back of the church for an usher to seat them. The usher offers his right arm to a woman guest, then leads her down the aisle to her seat. If she is accompanied by a man, he follows behind them.

The Timetable

Review the schedule for the next day. The ushers have been told to arrive one hour ahead of time to put their boutonnieres on and consult the seating plan which the head usher is in charge of. The bridegroom and his best man should arrive about half an hour later and go right into the vestry. Unless you and your bridesmaids are planning to dress at the church, club or hotel, you will arrive in cars about ten minutes before the service is scheduled to begin, your mother, your bridegroom's parents and the bridesmaids first, then you and your father or escort. It is nice to be able to dress right where the ceremony is to take place. That way you don't risk rumpling your gown on the way to the service. You should have the gowns delivered

Church Seating Arrangement

Church with Center Aisle

	Altar	
Bride's Side		Groom's Side

2 1		3 4

1—Bride's father
2—Bride's mother

3—Groom's father
4—Groom's mother

The bride's relatives and friends are seated on the left side of the church (facing the altar). The groom's relatives and friends on the right. If one will have a great many more than the other, the friends may be distributed so as to give a balanced appearance.

Church with Side Aisles

	Altar	
Bride's Side		Groom's Side

	1 2 4 3	

to the church and schedule your hairdresser and florist to meet you there for final arrangements. Allow yourself about two hours for dressing.

Since transportation is vital to the smooth running of the wedding, check your arrangements with the limousine service or scheduled driver friends well before the rehearsal. Make sure transportation has also been planned for out-of-town guests.

Time to Celebrate

After everyone has learned their part, it's time to relax and enjoy ... Traditionally, after the rehearsal, you and your groom, your parents, your attendants and their spouses, your clergy and spouse plus any out-of-town close relatives and friends you wish to include are invited by the groom's parents to the rehearsal dinner. It can be held anywhere, of course, but for the sake of ease the night before all the big festivities of the next day, it is often held in a restaurant and includes cocktails and either a buffet or sit-down dinner.

All the guests can, and should for the sake of fun, make toasts. Even the bride can make toasts to her fiance as the occasion demands. The toasts can be the best part of the evening.

Be sure it is an early evening, though. You need your sleep!

Partying

Before the rehearsal begins, many friends and relatives may want to entertain you and your groom. Your parents may host an engagement party and others may invite you and friends to celebrate at a tea, cocktail party, or dinner party.

The tea party is an informal, somewhat nostalgic, way to announce your engagement or to meet the older friends of either set of parents. If the tea is small, guests can be invited to come at a specified time. The hostess pours. For a larger tea, the invitations might read from three to five o'clock, or four until six o'clock. A receiving line is appropriate and should include your groom's mother. You should stand between your mother and your future mother-in-law. The hostess may invite close relatives or friends to pour for half-hour periods. Tea sandwiches and sweets are welcome accompaniments to the tea.

A cocktail party is more formal than a tea, but less expensive than a dinner party because hors d'oeuvres are all that is really needed. Cold or hot canapes, champagne for toasting, as well as the usual cocktails are a splendid celebration.

A formal dinner party or dinner dance is the most elegant of parties. Your hosts will be most generous to hold one for you. These parties are usually held in a club or hotel, but can be held at home if there is room. A buffet dinner is lovely for a smaller group. Here music, perhaps a pianist, is delightful.

Your bridesmaids and/or other female friends will hostess a shower or two. They may have decided on a theme shower, such as a kitchen, recipe, linen or lingerie shower, or if you need everything, have made it "generic." Appoint one guest as recorder as you open the gifts, so that you can thank everyone correctly. Another, especially your artistic friend, can collect the ribbons from the packages and slip them creatively through a hole in the center of a round piece of cardboard to form a bouquet for the rehearsal. Be sure to have someone take photographs or an audio or video cassette. This will be a valuable keepsake. A new "tradition" is to have both bride and groom and men and women to a shower, especially if they are not "teenagers." This can be a sophisticated adult party, with the whimsy of the gifts that will help you set up housekeeping.

A few days before the wedding itself, the bridesmaids will want to schedule a bridal luncheon, or you might want to treat them to this intimate occasion. This is a quiet time for you and your special friends to laugh together over old times and share hopes for the future. You can give them their gifts at this event.

The bachelor dinner is the men's time out. Either the ushers, the best man, or your groom himself can be the host. Your groom should give out his gifts at this time. The rest is left up to their imagination.

These are the preliminary parties. Now let's move on to the reception.

Flowers by Diane Love

Chapter 10
Planning the Reception

Time for Fun

"Today's bride wants the reception to reflect her style of entertaining," says Linda Galgay, senior account executive at Ridgewell's Caterer in Washington, D.C. "Brides used to want everything done by the etiquette book. Now they want to put their own personal style into the reception."

That is certainly understandable because the reception is the first official party you and your new husband will attend together. It will be your time to relax and enjoy yourselves after all the preparations and solemnity of the wedding service. Traditionally, your parents are hosts of the reception; but you and your fiance should be involved in the planning, too, right from the start.

Says Ms. Galgay, "At our first interview we work together to determine what the bride wants to *see* at her reception: people sitting down formally or lots of movement, for instance. Then we try to fit this 'look' into her chosen site and her budget."

Where it is and what you serve is determined by your lifestyle and the formality of the wedding, the time of the service, the budget, and the number of guests you want invited.

A morning wedding is usually followed by a breakfast, brunch, or luncheon. An afternoon wedding (from 1 p.m. to 4 p.m.) can be celebrated with a tea dance or light hors d'oeuvres and cocktails. A late afternoon or evening wedding is generally more formal and the reception should be a cocktail buffet or seated dinner.

Ridgewell's Ms. Galgay finds that in the Washington, D.C. area, most brides are choosing the cocktail buffet for their reception, even after the noon wedding. "They seem to prefer the flexibility a buffet offers," she says. "A buffet allows you to have more people in a smaller space, and it can be very formal or very informal depending on the food and decor."

Selecting the Site

Choose your site first and reserve it. The most popular party places are reserved up to a year in advance. So start right away.

In the previous chapters we discussed the type of decor that most flatters each color season. Winters, with your contrasting and dramatic coloring, look for a rather formal place with dark woods; shiny or silky fabrics; silver-toned metals; and clear, cool colors. How about a Georgian mansion, a hotel ballroom, starlit roof, museum or an historic theater? If your wedding is not that elaborate, look for a chic new restaurant or town club for your wedding celebration, or search among your friends for someone with a house that looks as glamorous as you feel.

Summers, you are looking for the stately and traditional place, with light-to-medium woods, antiques, fabrics with a soft sheen, silver-toned or rose-gold metals. Why not an historic townhouse, or formal rose garden, a country club, a university or military academy chapel?

Springs, with your spritely style, look for a place with light-to-medium woods, fabrics with a bright sheen, polished brass, and clear, warm colors. How about a restored plantation or fanciful Victorian house, a botanical garden, a restaurant filled with flowers, or a bright yellow-and-white tent dancing under the sky?

Autumns, you are the most natural and informal of the seasons and—weather permitting—will really glow in an outdoor setting, especially in the country. Look for a country inn, a restored farmhouse, even a park. Or go for a Tudor-style mansion, or a fun-loving ethnic restaurant, where you will be surrounded by those medium-to-dark woods, textured fabrics, and antique brass that become you so well.

Take the time to really search out your reception site. Tour your city and surrounding countryside. You'll have fun doing it. If you are considering a restaurant or hotel facility, eat there several times to make sure you really like the food and that the service is consistent. Just remember, if you are having an ultraformal or formal wedding, you will need space, a large room or suite of rooms, at the very least. You need space for a receiving line, food service, and probably dancing. The semiformal or informal wedding will require almost as much space if you have invited fifty or more guests, but you can also hold your reception in a less formal place, like the church parlor or reception room, a rented hall, or a comfortable restaurant.

If you like the idea of an old house and you don't have one readily available to you, consult your local historical society. Many times those under their care are rented out for a special event. An imaginative directory of "public places for private events and private places for public functions" is *Places* published by Tenth House Enterprises in New York City. Most of the places they list are in the metropolitan New York area, but listings in Boston, Philadelphia, Washington, D.C., Chicago, New Orleans, Houston, Los Angeles, and San Francisco are also included. Call 212-737-7536 for further information.

Clubs, hotels, and restaurants are often booked way in advance, so don't delay. Put down your deposit and reserve the date and time. Be sure to note all the equipment they are able to supply for the party: tables, chairs and tableware, waiters, clean-up crew, decoration props like vases and candlesticks, bar facilities. If they don't have these things and you need them, you'll have to arrange with the caterer and florist or friends and neighbors to get them. The rent you are charged for the site is also based on the amount of equipment that can be supplied there. Take this into consideration when you talk to your caterer.

The Menu

This is a party! The food must be something special, whether the wedding is breakfast for eight in your parents' home after a civil service, or dinner for five hundred in the grandest hotel in town after an ultraformal evening wedding. Unless you and your family have decided to provide the food yourselves or you are having the reception at a club, hotel, or restaurant where the food and beverages are the major part of the package, start looking for the caterer right away. Follow the same kinds of guidelines as you have for stationers and florists. Get recommendations from friends and acquaintances, interview several caterers and have them give you menu suggestions and a range of prices, check their references, then sign the contract. Caterers charge a per-person rate for both buffets and sit-down meals. Insist upon a written contract itemizing every service you will be paying for, including taxes and gratuities. The deposit is usually 50 percent with the balance due on the day of the wedding.

Linda Galgay warns brides to compare costs carefully. In Washington, D.C., for instance, caterers must provide liquor at the retail price. Hotels are allowed to mark up the price of liquor; and because it is frequently the item that provides most profit for them, it is significantly higher than what you would pay at a store. The food cost may be lower than the caterer's, but the liquor will be higher. In the Nation's Capital, the average catered reception costs about $40 to $50 per guest, including food, equipment, service and mixers (no liquor).

The caterer can provide everything from food and liquid refreshments to waiters and bartenders, tables and chairs, linens, tableware, including flatware, china and glasses (unless your reception site has these items). The caterer and staff will arrive some time early on the day of the wedding to begin setting up. If you and your family are doing all the cooking, consider hiring people to help serve and keep the tables full and clean up afterwards. This is a special party and you certainly will need to be out with the guests, cutting cake and dancing and enjoying yourself.

Your caterer will have many menu suggestions, from breakfast to dinner. At the end of this chapter you'll find sample menus prepared especially by Ridgewell's Caterer according to the personality of each season. But first, let's go over the basics.

The Wedding Breakfast, Brunch, or Luncheon

A wedding breakfast is served if your wedding takes place before 1 p.m. It can be as simple as eggs or as fancy as a light sit-down luncheon. After one, a full luncheon or buffet should be served. Officially, it is now called a reception. You will want to include an egg dish or meat, fruit, and/or a salad dish, breads, dessert, and beverages. For the wedding breakfast, coffee, tea, and juice may be all you need as beverages, but you will probably want champagne for one toast, at least. Since this is a celebration, alcoholic beverages may be served if you wish, but you should provide nonalcoholic beverages for those who don't drink. *Entertaining without Alcohol* by Dorothy Crouch (Acropolis Books, 1985) is filled with good ideas for delicious punches and cocktails.

The Afternoon Tea, Tea Dance, or Cocktail Buffet

The tea dance was very popular during World War II and seems to be making a comeback. Basically, it is an afternoon dance complete with hors d'oeuvres, tea sandwiches, and desserts, as well as the wedding cake. Tea, of course, is served, but other beverages, both alcoholic and nonalcoholic may be as well. A simple tea after an informal wedding ceremony would include everything but the music.

A cocktail buffet is a more elaborate party, appropriate for the afternoon or evening wedding. It consists of imaginative hors d'oeuvres, including sliced meats, fruits, cheeses, hot casseroles, whatever your caterer can come up with and your budget can afford, usually served on 8 inch plates. Alcoholic and nonalcoholic beverages are served. Your caterer may arrange different styles of food at "stations," such as those for Oriental foods, or vegetarian selections, or even Southwest dishes. Guests help themselves from the buffet tables and then sit at smaller tables, arranged around the reception room. The tables can be planned for "full seating," where tables are assigned and guests are seated all at one time; or "occasional seating," where smaller tables provide temporary seats for guests.

Champagne and a host of elegant hors d'oeuvres make a delightful afternoon reception. If your caterer needs more ideas, or you are doing the reception yourself, consult *Fast & Flashy Hors D'Oeuvres* by Michele Braden (Acropolis Books, 1988) for recipes you can prepare ahead of time and serve with flair.

The Seated Dinner for Hundreds or Just a Few Special Friends

Late afternoon and evening weddings are traditionally followed by a cocktail buffet or seated dinner. An elegant seated breakfast can follow the more formal morning weddings, and a seated luncheon for late morning or early afternoon (before 1 p.m.). Plan the menu with your caterer or family. You will need people to serve, whether hired waiters or appointed friends.

Actually, friends can help—and like to help—even when you have a trained staff to carry out the food preparation and service. Asking them to cut the wedding cake and help pass it; to serve tea, coffee, or punch; to supervise the signing of your guest book, these are all responsibilities for friends who are not serving as attendants but who might feel left out. Compile your list of these special helpers several weeks before the wedding and write a personal note to each asking them for their assistance.

The sit-down meal usually consists of hors d'oeuvres, including pastry, cheese and crackers, sliced meats, vegetables, relishes and/or fruits. A salad can be served before the main course or after with cheese. The main course should be something very special that you and your groom both like and that fits within your budget. Meat dishes, casseroles, fish, even pasta will fill the bill here. Breads, dessert, and beverages are also included. Usually the dessert is light, since you will also be serving wedding cake later on.

At large ultraformal and formal weddings, you should sit at the "Bride's Table" which is placed in a spot where all the guests can enjoy seeing you and your groom and attendants. Your table should be beautifully decorated and include place cards to tell your guests where each should sit. The spouses of your attendants can also be included at your table. Seat yourself and your groom in the center, you on his right. The best man should be on your right and the maid or matron of honor on your groom's. Next to the best man you can seat a bridesmaid or the minister's wife if they are included in your bridal group. The minister, then, should sit next to the maid of honor. Alternate bridesmaids and ushers around the rest of the table.

The parents may also have a special table—both your parents and your groom's. If the clergy and spouse are more your parents' age than yours, they can be seated more happily here. Relatives, honored guests, and other close friends are also seated here. Make place cards for this table too, seating your mother next to the groom's father in the center on one side, your father and the groom's mother opposite them. Alternate men and women around the rest of the table.

If your wedding is smaller, combine the two tables, seating yourself and groom in the center on one side, the best man on your right, the maid of honor on your groom's. On the other side of the table, in the center, should be your father and the mother of your groom, with the minister's wife to his right, the minister to her right. Next to the minister, on his right, your mother will sit. Next to the minister's wife on her right, a favorite relative or friend will sit. And so on around the rest of the table, men and women alternating.

Coloring the Reception

Winter French Service Menu

Chinese Pancakes Filled with
Icy Pink Shrimp, Bay Scallops, Water Chestnuts,
Snow Pea Pods and Pimento

Tournedos of Beef
Fois Gras
Black Truffle Essence
Chestnut Mousse in Pastry Baskets
Bouquetiere of Winter Vegetables

Celery Root Remoulade with Arugula, Radicchio,
Shaved Marinated Peppers and
Sun Dried Black Olives
Asagio Toasts

Dipped Grapes, Chocolate Palmiers,
Raspberry Marzipan Dates, Crystallized Pineapple,
Roasted Walnuts and Silver Almonds

WHITE SATIN BRIDAL CAKE

White Chocolate Cake
Filled and Iced with White Chocolate Buttercream,
Wrapped in White Fondant and
Decorated with Pulled Sugar Ribbons

Groom's cake
Florentine Genoise Brushed with Cognac,
Filled and Frosted with Chocolate Ganache, Decorated with
Praline, Chocolate Leaves and Curls

Summer a la Russe Menu

Hors d'Oeuvres

Canápes

Carrot Vichyssoise
Chive Tuilles

Medallions of Plume de Veau
with Chanterelle Butter
Pecan Risotto with Sun Dried Cherries
Sugar Snap Peas with Mint

Composed Salad
Basil Vinaigrette

Summer Berries with
Sabayon

Amethyst Wedding Cake

Pound Cake Brushed with Grand Marnier
and Raspberry Jam,
Filled and Iced in Vanilla Buttercream
Decorated with Pink Roses and Lilacs

Petit Fours
Wedding Mints

Autumn Brunch Menu

HORS D'OEUVRES

Scallion Pancakes with Shredded Duck Breast
and Tomato Chutney
Baby Backfin Crab Cakes on Herb Toasts with
Lemon Caper Tartar Sauce
Wild Mushroom Pockets

Pumpkin Cheddar Soup with Toasted Pumpkin Seed
Red Pepper Cornbread

Grilled Chicken and Country Ham on Southern Biscuits
Orange Hollandaise
Pastry Cornucopia Spilling Baby Vegetables
Spinach and Artichoke Creme Fraîche
Apple Walnut Muffins Filled with Smoked Turkey and Sherry Mustard

Wheels of Brie Garnished with Fall Apricots and
Champagne Grapes
Nutmeat Pate and Wheat Crackers
Peppered Popovers

HARVEST WEDDING CAKE

Spiced Cake Tiers Filled with Ginger Marmalade,
Cream Cheese Frosting,
Set in a Grapevine Wreath
Decorated with Seasonal Fruit and Dried Flowers
Bird's Nest Cookies

Spring Luncheon Buffet Menu

Norwegian Smoked Salmon
Lemon Coriander Sauce
Lemon Wedges
Capers
Heart Shaped Iverson Toasts

Asparagus Spears Wrapped in Buckwheat Crepes
Champagne Sauce

Crabmeat and Artichoke Flan

Poached Gingered Fruits
Apricot Yogurt Sauce

Kringle Hearts
Brioche
Sweet Butter
Nasturtium Jelly

GOLDEN YELLOW WEDDING CAKE

Heart Shaped Tiers of Florentine Sponge
Filled with Almond Cream,
Iced in Lemon Buttercream and Decorated
with Roasted Hazelnuts and Almonds,
Lemon Leaves and Lemon Thyme

Noisette Heart Cookies

Coloring the Reception

The Wedding Cake

Every wedding must have a wedding cake. A beautiful tiered cake, displayed on its own table at the center of your reception, is a decoration that will draw admiring guests and be the focal point when you and your groom cut the first piece together, as friends and family toast your happiness.

The French, of course, created the layered marvels of today. Before that, wedding guests were served little sugared cakes. Greek couples shared a sesame cake, the symbol of fertility, while the Romans started their ceremony with an offering of wheat cake, crumbled over the wedding couples' heads. Today's cakes are truly magnificent.

Again, ask your friends for recommendations for the best baker in town, then visit each for a prewedding tasting. Your caterer may also provide the cake, but it is better to go to a baker who specializes in wedding cakes. Each one is a masterpiece and the baker should be proud of his or her confections. Some couples also have a groom's cake, which is smaller and set next to the wedding cake. The groom's cake is traditionally a fruitcake. Until the 18th century, when finely ground flour and baking powder were introduced in America, the wedding cake was a dark fruitcake. Now it is white and the groom's cake is dark. Let your baker know how many guests you've invited. Cakes are bought by the pound, and range from one to seven dollars per serving. Some clubs include the cake in their per-head price. Be sure you get their baker's name and do the tasting and flavor selction. Don't take anything for granted.

Your wedding cake should be decorated in your seasonal palette to complement your color scheme. Winters in white, have your cake iced in white. Summers, Springs and Autumns, your icing should be off-white, just like your dress. A tiny tinge of food color can be added if you wish: blue, pink, or violet for Winters and Summers; yellow, peach, aqua, or periwinkle for Autumns and Springs. These colors should certainly appear in the sugar-dough decorations, which can range from very delicate flowers to fanciful cupids. Capture the feeling of your wedding in your selection. Ribbons and fresh flowers, like those you and your maids are carrying, also carry through the theme.

Flowers can be tucked into a vase on top of the cake, around each tier and on the cake table itself; but traditionally a tiny bride and groom appear there. If you're a blonde Summer, or a red-headed Spring or Autumn, don't choose brunette figures for the top of your cake.

Coloring the Reception

If your maids are wearing pink, or white with pink or peach underskirts and sashes, and carrying pink or peach flowers, your cake could be decorated with pink or peach flowers, too. If you are a dramatic Winter, staging a black and white wedding, your cake can be all white decorated with silver.

Inside there are no traditions. Taste the kinds of cake your baker can concoct: yellow, almond, and pound cakes, chocolate fudge, carrot, lemon, hazelnut, spice or orange—filled with chocolate, pistachio, marzipan, raspberry puree, mocha cream. I'm sure you'll enjoy this part of planning the wedding. You may even want to have a tasting party with your groom and attendants to judge the best flavor.

Some brave brides or their mothers make the masterpiece themselves. Martha Stewart's *Weddings* (Clarkson N. Potter, 1987) has some marvelous recipes and ideas for decorations, as does the *Rose Levy Beranbaum Cake Book* (William Morrow & Co., 1988).

Many weddings feature a groom's cake as well. This smaller cake is displayed next to the wedding cake. "Brides often plan the groom's cake to reflect his personality," says Linda Galgay of Ridgewell's. "I've seen them with basketball nets or ethnic themes." This is the fun cake. It is an optional expense, but can be part of the fun of the wedding and is cut and passed to guests as a memento of your day together.

Timing

Linda Galgay advises brides to count on about four hours for the average wedding: half hour for the service; 45 minutes to one hour for passing hors d'oeuvres at the reception, one-and a-half to two hours for eating, and about half an hour to one hour for the cake-cutting and champagne toasts.

Embellishments

Photographers and Photographs. Most of the portraits will be taken before the ceremony, during it (if your church allows) and immediately afterward, before the receiving line begins. During the reception, your official photographer and friends should look for the fun and action—people dancing, talking in small groups, the receiving line, toasts, cutting the cake, you tossing the bouquet to the unmarried women, your first dance, your new husband removing your garter and tossing it to the unmarried men, your attendants decorating the getaway car, you and your husband dashing away into your new life together. Sometimes, the pictures taken by your dear old friends, who know you so well, will be even better than the photographer's. These are the relaxed photographs that show the people you love having a good time. They are very special. Be sure to give your photographer a list of the people and events you don't want him or her to miss on film.

Music and Musicians. From records to an orchestra, it doesn't matter how big or small your wedding is, the reception is the place for your favorite music. But don't forget the ages of your other guests and include music they'll like, too. If there is no room for dancing but you want some soothing background music, a musician playing the piano, or a harp, or a strolling violin can be a lovely addition. The basic trio of piano, bass, and drums takes up little room and can provide a great deal of music—from classical through modern. And, if there is a strong ethnic background in your family, by all means have your musicians play the music your family enjoys.

Again, ask your friends and acquaintances for suggestions. Call the local musicians' union or music school and get of list of groups playing in the area. Go listen to them and interview their leaders. Or ask for an audiocassette and "audition" them at home on your tape recorder. Prepare a list of the kind of music you and your groom like and discuss your selections.

You'll want something special for your first dance with your new husband and with your father. Then a selection of dance music when everyone else joins in. You might want a particular song for the cake cutting, another for when you toss your bouquet, and another when you and your groom leave the reception.

Get an estimate from each musical group. Consider it carefully. Discuss what they will wear and make sure it is appropriate. Then make your choice and sign the contract. Be sure the contract spells out exactly what you will be getting for your money—how long they'll be playing, what equipment they'll bring, what equipment you have to supply, and so on.

Decorations and Decorators. The decorations for the reception carry on the theme of your wedding. Plan these with your florist and the manager of the reception hall and your parents. You may need flowers for the buffet and guest tables and flowers for the bride's table, flowers around the cake table and on the cake itself and on the cake knife. These should, of course, be in your seasonal palette and pick up on some of the flowers from the ceremony. Sometimes you can have the flowers from the ceremony brought to the reception.

You and your florist should survey the reception site together and discuss where you want decorations—garlands on a staircase or mantel in a home, tall plants decorated with tiny white lights, banks of potted plants around the bandstand. Your budget and your theme should stimulate your imagination. You have chosen your reception site because it reflects your style. The decorations, whether they are flowers or balloons, should enhance your theme. If you are having a sit-down meal, keep the arrangements low enough for guests to see each other across the table. Napkins and china must blend. To be safe, Summers, Springs, and Autumns use cream-colored linens with pastels, while Winters use white with bright flowers. Caterers will show you their linen and tableware books so you can make your selections.

Bridal napkins and other decorative keepsakes, like individual wedding cake boxes, with your names and the date of your wedding or your monograms must be ordered through your bridal consultant or department or specialty shop several weeks in advance.

Candles are always a lovely addition to tables and mantels, but use them only for late afternoon or evening receptions. They are not appropriate earlier in the day.

The Receiving Line

You ultraformal, formal and even semiformal brides who wanted a big wedding, now is your turn to greet all the guests and thank them personally for their gift, if you brief yourself ahead of time and can remember. The receiving line should be formed as soon as the wedding party arrives at the reception after the photographer has finished the wedding group pictures. Or it can be held at the wedding site before the photographs are taken. Drinks and hors d'oeuvres may be served to the guests while they are waiting for the line to be formed.

If you are having a very large wedding of more than 200 guests, you should appoint a friend, relative, or catering official as the announcer who asks the name of each guest as he or she reaches the head of the receiving line, and tells your mother so she can begin the introductions. She greets the guest by name, then turns either to the groom's father if he is in the line or to his mother and introduces the guest, and so on down the line.

Positions in the receiving line are...

1. Announcer

2. Bride's mother

3. Groom's father (if he is from out-of-town and will want to meet guests)

4. Groom's mother

5. Bride's father (if your groom's father is in the line)

6. Bride

7. Groom

8. The maid or matron of honor

9. , 10., 11., 12., etc. Your bridesmaids in the order they walked down the aisle.

You, and the mothers and bridesmaids, should wear your gloves during the receiving line, but the men may remove theirs. Your rector or rabbi may stand in the receiving line if you wish, between you and your father. The best man, ushers, and other attendants do not need to be with you.

Toasting

One of the most delightful traditions at a wedding is toasting. At a formal wedding the toast is proposed when the bridal couple are first seated or right after the dessert before the cake is cut. At a semiformal or informal wedding, it can be given after the receiving line or before the cake cutting.

The best man makes the first toast to you and your groom. He may simply say, "Here's to the most beautiful of brides," as he raises his glass, or he makes a lengthier toast, drawing on some favorite childhood story or memory of the two of you. Then all in the group, except for the bride, raise their glasses and take a sip. If the toast is dedicated to both the bride and groom, then you both remain seated.

Your new husband should then rise and thank his best man for both of you. He can propose a special toast to you at this point. Other members of the wedding party and both fathers are welcome to rise and propose toasts, as they are inspired. Congratulatory telegrams may also be read at this time.

The First Dance

I remember our first dance. We had requested the "Blue Danube Waltz," completely forgetting that my husband did not know how to waltz. There we were on the dance floor in front of all the guests, and the music began to play . . . Drifting into the rhythm, I started counting . . . 1, 2, 3 . . . 1, 2, 3, all the way around 2, 3 . . . and we were waltzing. Some of the best pictures were of that first magic dance.

After a few turns around the floor alone, your groom should ask his mother to dance while your father or another close male relative dances with you. Then your new husband gallantly dances with your mother while you dance with his father. Then everyone joins in the dancing.

Cutting the Cake

Soon it is time to cut your beautiful wedding cake. The crowd is gathered around the cake table, you slice the first piece while your husband guides your hand, he gives you a bite and you give him one. Everyone laughs and applauds. The rest of the cake is then sliced and served to the guests.

If your reception is a champagne and dessert type occasion, have the cake ceremony before the receiving line, then your guests may have a slice as they move into the reception area for punch and other refreshments.

If yours is a seated dinner or luncheon, you should cut the first slice of your wedding cake together right before the dessert course.

Tossing the Bouquet

Now you must leave your bridal flowers to the next bride in line. Some brides order a smaller replica of their bouquet for this special tradition, so they can keep their real bouquet as a keepsake. Whatever flowers you throw, your bridesmaids and unmarried friends will have fun surrounding you, as you with your back turned, twirl around and toss them into the crowd. It is said that whoever catches the bouquet will be the next bride.

Next, your new husband helps you remove the special garter right above your right knee. He turns his back, twirls around, and tosses it to the assembled ushers and bachelors. Whoever catches this lacy garment is to be the next groom.

Going Off . . .

At last, you can sneak off to change your clothes. The party goes on now, without you and your groom, although your bridesmaids and his ushers may have been up to mischief, decorating the car or playing other pranks. We'll let you discover what they've been up to yourself!

In the meantime, both of you slip off to separate rooms to change, then re-emerge dressed in your lovely "going away" costumes. The best man should have put your luggage in the car and have gone to bring it around to the front door.

The guests are given small bags of birdseed or paper rose petals, tied with satin ribbon. As you descend the stairs or approach the door, they gently toss their greetings on you as you run for the car. And you are off . . .

Coloring the Reception

Chapter 11
The Wedding Gifts A Colorful Lot

Getting Your New Home Started

The wedding gifts you are about to receive are loving contributions to a new life for you and your fiance. Each gift will be thoughtfully chosen by someone who cares about you and wants their gift to be part of your home.

Traditional wedding gifts are dinnerware, flatware, glassware, or linens. They are sent to the bride's home by your friends and family after they receive a wedding invitation. In a way, they are your modern "dowry," because they are what the two of you will be eating, sleeping, bathing, and drinking from for a long time.

Your family, friends, and acquaintances appreciate help in selecting what you and your fiance want for your life together. That's what the Bridal Registry is all about. This is a service provided by fine department, jewelry, and specialty stores. After you have selected your china, flatware, crystal, and bed and table linen, register your choices with the store. Whenever a friend comes in or calls in to order, they consult this Bridal Registry to see what others have bought you already and what you still need. Some registries are computerized and national. Wherever that store has a branch, they have you on file, so your friends from around the country can give you just what you need. Others are local, but if you let your friends and relatives know where you are registered, they can call from anywhere in the country and place an order.

So as soon as you set the date, confirm the church and reception place, take the time to shop—with your fiance. Take your time and choose carefully. These are purchases that last a lifetime.

Start with Color

Take your palette with you when you shop together, especially for your tableware. And consider your lifestyle, too. Are you ultraformal, formal, semiformal, or informal in your outlook? More importantly, will you always be? Many young couples make the mistake of not choosing silver and china, thinking they will never use it. But later on, you may want to entertain more formally. Choose now. With even a few pieces of china and silver, you have a beginning on dinnerware you'll appreciate long into the future.

The basic rule when selecting patterns for your dinnerware, glassware, and flatware is to choose two patterned and one plain, or two plain and one patterned. In other words, you may select dinnerware and silver with elaborate patterns and a very simple, elegant stemware; or, an elaborate silver pattern with plain dinner and glassware.

Formal Dinnerware

Start with your dinnerware because its color and pattern dominate any table. Winters, you'll be looking for plain white china or plain white with silver trim, or with a contrasting colored border (from your palette) and a silver rim. Summers, look for off-white china with a soft floral pattern in pastels from your palette. Don't be too timid, however, and choose something that is very insipid. You'll get tired of it as your tastes become more sophisticated. Springs, you should go with off-white china, too, but look for an animated floral pattern in your seasonal colors. Autumns, oyster white is the background color for your dinnerware, trimmed with gold, leaves and other botanical embellishments, or a geometric border.

Dinnerware is usually sold by the place setting. But *open stock* means that individual pieces of a pattern may be purchased separately. It doesn't mean that a store will always have every piece in that pattern, but they can order it for you as long as the manufacturer is still making it. Popular patterns may be manufactured for twenty years or more, others for only two or three years.

A basic place setting consists of a dinner plate, dessert/salad plate, a bread and butter plate, and a cup and saucer. Sometimes soup bowls are substituted in the five-piece dinner service for the bread and butter plate. Aim for twelve place settings for the days when you are in charge of Thanksgiving dinners, but be happy if you receive eight place settings to start your new life with. You'll be able to invite three other couples to join you and your husband for dinner in style in your new home.

Dinnerware is also sold in *closed sets*. This means you must purchase the entire group of dinnerware in that pattern, packaged by the manufacturer at a lower price than purchasing individual pieces or place settings. The most common sets today are for four, eight, or twelve place settings. There are also services for four called *starter sets*. These are usually only available in earthenware or more casual china.

Other dinnerware pieces available in most patterns are the open vegetable dish, sauce boat with stand, covered vegetable dish, demitasse cup and saucer, service platters, bouillon cups and stands, cream soup and lug soup (with one handle), fruit dish, sugar bowl with lid, and cream pitcher. Some of your friends may want to give you one of these pieces.

You don't really need a complete set of your fine china because all the pieces will rarely be used together in a formal setting. In fact, don't feel you have to select everything in the same pattern. Some manufacturers have designed dinner services with mix-and-match motifs, plain borders on some, floral on others, for instance. Or choose a dinner service in one pattern, dessert plates in another. Just be sure they blend, and they will if you use your seasonal colors.

Style refers to the uniform shape of the china, whether the plates are round or octagonal or even square. The *pattern* means the decorative design and colors of the dinnerware. The word *china* is commonly used today to describe all types of dinnerware. Originally, of course, it meant the fine, translucent porcelain imported from China to Europe, beginning in the sixteenth century. Fine china was not even made in Europe until about 200 years ago when the English mastered the techniques of the Orient. The English called even their own porcelain *chinaware,* and eventually it was shortened to china. Today most fine department and jewelry stores feature a china section where everything from bone china to earthenware is sold.

All china is ceramic which means it is made from clay and baked. But there are several different kinds, and you should be aware of the differences as you decide upon a pattern. *Porcelain* is the very finest china. If you hold a porcelain dinner plate up to the light, and put your hand behind it, you will be able to see your hand's shadow because porcelain, and all fine china, is translucent.

English *bone china* contains a mixture of ox bone ash which gives it a characteristic whiteness and translucency. If you compare bone china with all other types of porcelain, you will immediately see this whiteness. The body of most china has an off-white, grayish cast, except for some American china which is ivory.

There are many famous English bone china makers: Wedgwood, Royal Worcester, Royal Crown Derby, Royal Doulton, to name a few. The quality of French porcelain is as good as any other fine china made today. Limoges china is from the town of the same name in the heart of French porcelain manufacturing. Bernadaud, Ceralene, and Haviland china are made there. Richard Ginori is the only major porcelain manufacturer in Italy. Ginori china is as fine as any on the market. The German firms of Rosenthal and Arzberg make a very fine china. Royal Copenhagen is the only major manufacturer of fine china in Scandinavia. Their designs and styling are unique and unmistakable. From Japan, the largest single manufacturer of dinnerware in the world, comes a wide variety of china with much variety in quality. Noritake manufactures the very finest china. Lenox is the most famous name in china manufacturing in this country.

Earthenware

Some people think that china is very fragile and should only be used for very special occasions and holidays. Actually, it is stronger than other ceramics available in tableware. Earthenware seems more solid, but it is made from coarser clay and baked at lower temperatures. It is more porous than china, therefore, and chips easily. On the other hand, earthenware comes in vivid colors and designs. Just check for high quality earthenware that has been fired at higher temperatures.

Italians make bright-colored, boldly designed earthernware patterns. Theirs is not as durable as English or French, but it is less expensive and very colorful.

Ironstone

Stronger than earthenware, ironstone must meet government standards of firing and clay quality in order to legally qualify for the name *ironstone*. It comes in a wide variety of traditional styles and colors, and does not chip as easily as earthenware.

Stoneware

Stoneware looks like earthenware but has the durability of china. It is rather heavy in appearance, making it a much less formal dinnerware. But casual lifestyles today have made it popular. In recent years potters have developed a process of covering the stoneware with a white glaze and applying designs that make it resemble fine china. Stoneware, too, must meet strict government standards to be called stoneware.

The Scandinavians are especially noted for their excellent stoneware. Manufacturers like Rorstrands and Gustavesberg in Sweden are famous for their ceramic arts in informal, modern designs.

Silverplate

Every serving piece available in china is also made in silver or silverplate. Tea and coffee services come in silver. You may prefer china, but silver is a better choice. Silver is certainly as elegant as china and it will always coordinate with any china pattern. If you keep your investment in china down, you can add to the pattern you choose now as your budget expands or even start a new pattern without guilt. Start now with dinner plates, soup plates, bread and butter plates for your dinner service, and salad plates and cups and saucers for your dessert service.

Daily Dinnerware

For everyday use, you will need more dinnerware than for formal service. Every meal makes different demands. A breakfast set, for instance, can be different from the rest of your dinnerware. It isn't that expensive and will relieve the boredom of eating from the same plates morning, noon, and night. And, your everyday dinnerware can be porcelain, stoneware, ironware, or earthenware. It's up to you, your lifestyle, your budget, and your decorating scheme. There is a "casual" china which is now manufactured as an outgrowth of commercial grade china, required by law for use by restaurants. It comes in a wide variety of colors and styles and ranges from moderately expensive to inexpensive. You'll want to list your choice for everyday dinnerware on the bridal registry, too. Many friends will decide to make their gifts be something you'll use every day. This is also a more affordable gift for those shoppers on tight budgets.

Flatware

Unlike china or stemware, most of the silver sold in this country is made here. A large part is manufactured in the New England area by such firms as Gorham, Reed & Barton, Towle, Oneida, and Lunt; and in the Middle Atlantic states by firms such as Kirk Stieff. The industry developed in the Northeast and Middle Atlantic states since the days of the colonial silversmiths.

Your flatware may be sterling silver, vermeil, silverplate, pewter, pewterplate, sterling II, or stainless steel.

A beautiful sterling silver place setting could cost about twice as much as your china place setting and three to five times as much as your stemware. The selection of your silver pattern is, therefore, the one you and your fiance will want to take the most time over. You will be living with it for a long, long time. Some experts recommend choosing your silver first, since it cannot be changed with ease like glassware or china, and should, these experts advise, never be selected just to go with your china. It should stand on its own.

Sterling silver by law is 92.5 parts pure silver to 7.5 parts alloy. Be sure to check for the word "sterling" stamped on every piece. Less expensive sterling knives are sometimes hollow. When buying silver, be sure to note whether your pattern is available in open stock. If it is, you will always be able to get it. When a silver company "discontinues" a pattern, it simply deactivates it. Usually, once a year, all manufacturers announce that they will take orders for all inactive patterns. Because of the way silver is made, it is easy for a manufacturer to continue a popular pattern, since they preserve the original dies.

Silver can be engraved, embossed, etched, hammered, or chased. In engraving, the pattern is incised or cut into the piece. You should decide whether or not you want your silver engraved with your monogram: either yours and your husband's first initials on either side of a larger surname initial, or your first and maiden name initial on either side of a larger new surname initial. In embossing, the pattern is raised. This technique is used for border decorations. Etching is rarely used because it is too expensive. Hammering is done by machine to produce a hand-wrought look. Repousse is similar to embossing and used for border decorations. It produces very ornate silver, with an overall pattern or design. Chasing is the process of tracing a design into the silver with a sharp tool. Chased trays are very popular because the surface pattern hides scratches. Patterns with intricate designs are more costly than simpler designs.

Silver finishes can be shiny or matte. A shiny finish is polished and buffed by machine. The matte or butler finish is done with brushes and a very fine pumice stone. Winters will prefer the shiny finish, while her soft Summer friends will probably choose a matte finish.

Vermeil is even more expensive than silver because it is sterling silver plated with 24-karat gold. It is available in a wide variety of patterns and in holloware. Jackie Kennedy popularized vermeil when she selected it for use at state dinners during her husband John's presidency.

Because of the high prices of sterling and vermeil, list all your pieces in the bridal registry but note that you really want only knives, forks, and teaspoons now. You can always add salad forks, dessert spoons, butter knives, and serving pieces over countless birthdays and holidays.

Less expensive than sterling silver and vermeil are:

- silverplate which is made of a non-ferrous metal then electroplated with pure silver;

- pewter, which is a soft, silver-gray metal made of tin alloys;

- pewterplate, a base metal electroplated with pewter;

- sterling II, which means sterling handles and stainless steel tines, blades, and bowls; and

- stainless steel, a nonprecious metal available with satin, mirror, and new pewter finishes.

Select with care and check whether the fork tines are too blunt or too sharp. Pay attention to the weight of these alloys; the heavier the piece, the better the quality and durability.

There are literally hundreds of patterns to choose from, but there are just a few styles upon which they are all based:

- American Colonial - with a fiddleback handle, sometimes with a shell design,

- English Chippendale - curved at the base of the handle and decorated with varying degrees of curved scrolls at the base,

- Baroque - curved at the sides and the base of the handle with elaborate designs at sides and base,

- French Provincial - curved at the base of the handle and sides and decorated with simple designs at sides and base,

- Modern - simple, clean lines and no decoration whatsoever—and,

- Contemporary - basically modern in shape but with a simple design along one side of the handle.

What You'll Need

Armed with this information ahead of time, you can zip right through the bridal registry process. Take a moment to "digest" the following. It will make you feel 100% smarter when you begin your selections.

There are two kinds of utensils you need to be concerned with:

- flatware - the actual utensils you eat with—from sterling to stainless—and,

- hollowware - the pieces you serve with.

Hollowware includes candlesticks, salt and pepper shakers, bowls, trays, platters, gravy boat and tray, sauce bowl and tray, chafing dishes, and your tea and coffee services.

Flatware prices are usually quoted by five-piece place setting which includes a place-size fork, a place-size knife, a salad fork, a cream soup spoon or a butter spreader, and a teaspoon. Three-piece settings are popular today, as they are more affordable for the gift-giver. They include knife, fork, and spoon.

A dinner-size fork and knife are often available (check your pattern) and cost a little more because they are larger. The place-size knife and fork are in between dinner- and luncheon-sized utensils. The dinner size is about 3/4 of an inch larger and the luncheon size 1/2 of an inch smaller. If you are an ultraformal or formal-type entertainer, or think you will become one, choose the dinner size. The luncheon or place size is adequate for most informal hostesses.

There are usually two shapes of butter spreader from which to choose, and you can select the flat handle or a hollow one. It's simply a matter of taste, since the price is usually about the same. You may also have to choose between a dessert spoon and a soup spoon in your basic place setting. The difference is simply in the shape of the spoon's bowl. The cream soup spoon has a round bowl, the dessert spoon has an oval one. Dessert spoons may be more versatile, since they can be used for most kinds of soup as well as dessert. If you are buying cream soup bowls in your china pattern, however, you may wish to select soup spoons in your flatware as well. Aim for twelve place settings, but be happy with four to six to start.

Once you have your basic pieces, you can begin to collect all the others: coffee spoons and iced beverage spoons; cocktail forks and ice cream forks; steak, fork and fish knives; serving spoons, gravy ladle, cold meat fork, and sugar spoon and sugar tongs; cake or pie server, olive or pickle fork. Whatever your pattern, there are beautiful serving pieces to accompany it.

Glassware

There's more to glassware than drinking. Glassware can be blown or pressed. Blown glass is the lightest, thinnest, clearest of glass and the most expensive, since its beauty depends upon the skill of the glass blower. Until recently, all fine glassware was handblown. Now a few of the better quality glass manufacturers have been able to substitute computers as blowers. Pressed glass is the result of hand or machine labor. It is heavier and simpler in design than blown glass.

You can choose from cut, etched, or engraved glassware, decorated with brushed or stamped gold or platinum. Cut glass takes a great deal of skill to create and is, therefore, the most expensive of glassware.

The color in colored glass comes from the mixture that is blown. It can be formal or informal, depending on the design you choose. A colored glass usually costs more than plain glass because more materials are used to create it.

In addition to clear glass, there are two types of opaque glassware: milk glass and opaline. The whiteness of the chemical mixture used for the blowing makes milk glass opaque. It is less formal than clear glass and blends easily into Early American or country settings. Opaline, which is also milky in appearance, is semi-opaque and more formal. It is handblown and much more expensive.

Lustreware is another kind of glass in which chemicals are used to achieve an irridescent effect. The colors are sprayed on and are not part of the composition of the glass, but they are colorfast. Lustreware is transparent and is used in formal settings only.

What You'll Need

There are three categories of glassware: drinking glasses, serving pieces, and decorative objects. What you need to get started are drinking glasses, coordinated with your china and flatware patterns. A crystal suite consists of a water goblet, wine glass, and champagne glass (flute or dessert/champagne). An iced-beverage glass may be substituted for the water goblet.

Drinking glasses are divided into two groups: stemware and barware. Stemware is used to serve beverages at the table; while the other is used for serving bar beverages.

Stemware goes with your fine china. You'll need goblets, and wine, sherbert or champagne, cocktail, and cordial glasses. A goblet is used for water and holds from nine to twelve ounces. It is the largest glass.

The wine glass is a smaller version of the goblet. Wine connoisseurs will say you need several different glasses to truly bring out the special bouquet and flavor of wines. And if you plan to serve wine frequently, you should investigate the different shapes. It is perfectly acceptable, however, to have one kind of wine glass. The red wine glass is the largest. It holds eight ounces, has a globelike bowl and is appropriate for all red wines except port and sherry. It is sometimes the only size available in the wine glass for a stemware pattern. A white wine glass holds only six ounces and has a narrower bowl. Use it for all white wines except Rhine wine. The Rhine wine glass is taller than a white wine glass but has a similar shaped bowl.

The sherbert or dessert/champagne glass is always shorter and more shallow than the goblet. It is almost twice as wide, however, so is perfect for desserts such as ice cream and sherbert, as well as champagne celebrations.

Cocktail glasses are shorter than the average wine glass and have a wider opening. Even though cocktails should not be served at the dinner table, these glasses are considered part of your stemware.

The cordial glass, like the cocktail glass, is never used at the table, but is considered part of your stemware. There are many different kinds of after-dinner drinks and almost every one of them has its own specially shaped glass. To get you started in your entertaining, choose the one in your pattern you like best. Add others as you can.

These are the only glasses you really need in your expensive stemware, although juice and footed iced tea glasses are frequently part of the pattern's offerings. The footed iced tea is usually on a short, low stem and has a larger capacity than the water goblet. The juice glass is either on a stem or on a flat bottom. You can also use your white wine glasses for juice for brunch or lunch. Wine, goblet, and dessert/saucer champagne glasses are all you really need now. The cost of eight of each of these three glasses will be just a little more than for one place setting of your sterling silver, depending on your pattern and manufacturer. Yet glassware, tall and sparkling, can pull silver and china together into a glittering table ensemble you'll be proud to display for years to come.

If you get into barware now, or if you decide to select less expensive glassware instead of stemware, you'll find a complete range of sizes, including goblets, wine glasses, and sherberts. Ice-tea glasses, tumblers, whiskey and soda glasses, old-fashioned glasses, tall pilsners, beer goblets and mugs, and assorted cocktail glasses are all available.

Linens

Once upon a time linens were an integral part of the bride's trousseau. Today they are more appropriately listed with your wedding gifts in your bridal registry. You'll need linens for your bed, your bath, and your table. As always, take your palette with you when you make your selections. Consider the formality of your lifestyle, especially when it comes to table linens. And don't forget the colors of things you can't change, like bathroom tiles or the kitchen floor in a rented apartment, when you choose your linens. They can accent or intensify unfortunate tiles, linoleum, or wood finishes.

The J.P. Stevens Co., one of the country's largest producers of bed and bath linens, recommends three fitted and three flat sheets for each bed, three pillow cases for each pillow and two pillows for each head. They advise you to have two mattress pads, one winter and one summer blanket for each bed, a comforter and bedspread or a quilted reversible bedspread that can double as a comforter, and a bedskirt if you are using a duvet or comforter instead of a spread.

You can judge the quality of sheets by examining their thread count, or the number of threads per square inch of fabric. The more threads there are, the better the quality, and the softer the sheet will feel. Percale sheets made of all cotton or a cotton and polyester blend are easy to care for and require no ironing. Top quality percale, made of 100% combed cotton, has a 200 to 250 thread count. They have the same feel as old-fashioned cotton sheets. There are even luxurious no iron satin sheets and chill-fighting flannel sheets from which to choose. You can use sheets not only on your bed but as an inexpensive fabric for tables, walls, screens, and upholstering. More information on decorating with sheets is in the next chapter.

For your bathroom, Stevens recommends two bath mats, two shower curtains and liners; three bath towels, three hand towels, three body sheets, six wash cloths, and three fingertip towels per person. Towels come in sheared, terry, and velour, with plain, flat side-to-side woven cam borders or flat horizontal geometric design dobby borders. Look for quality in your towels, too. They receive more use than almost any of your linens.

Table Linens

Your table linens will be the backdrop for all your beautiful new tableware. They contain the background colors upon which everything else will sit, so choose with your tableware palette in mind. Some fabrics are more formal than others. Linen, cotton, polyester, ramie, polyester/linen, polyester/cotton, polyester/ramie and acrylic are available in cloths for tables that seat four or sixteen.

You'll need several tablecloths, place mats, and napkins to get started: for breakfast for just the two of you, two placemats and three napkins (one for keeping rolls or toast warm); for lunch, brunch, and informal dinner entertaining, a 52-inch square or 52 x 70-inch oval cloth and four to six 17-inch napkins are ideal; for formal dinner entertaining, a large damask, linen, lace or embroidered cloth and 24-inch square matching napkins.

Table mats are also very acceptable now for formal entertaining; and they come in a variety of fabrics and materials, from mirrors to linens. Table linens are fun to change with the seasons or your moods. They are a relatively inexpensive way to "dress up" or "dress down" your table.

Adding Your Initials

Whether on your flatware or your linens, many brides like to have their initials or monogram put onto gifts. Traditionally, your married surname initial is etched onto your flatware or embroidered on your linens above, below or between the first and last initials of your maiden name. For example, Helen Osborn marrying Jim Brown would use the monogram: B above or below her own H O

B
HO

Sometimes Jim's first initial and Helen's may be placed above the B.

JH
B

Now, if you have decided to retain your maiden name after your marriage, monogramming is no longer an easy decision to make. Both sets of initials may be used if you both buy the flatware or towel, but use yours alone if the gifts come from many relatives and friends.

Registering Your Choices

Now that you know what everything is called, be sure to visit your department or specialty stores, and register your gift choices. The sales staffs will be pleased to help you and your fiance fill out the forms. In Chapter 12 is a checklist of what you will need and most importantly, what you have already received from friends and relatives. Use it to describe the gift, the giver's name and address, where it was purchased, and when you wrote the thank-you note.

Now let's put all these beautiful things into your new home.

A Glossary of Wedding Gift Terms

Bed Coverings

Bedskirt   A covering for the lower part of a bed, extending from under the mattress to the floor and used to conceal bed frame and legs.

Comforter   Soft, warm bed covering with a light and puffy filling, usually of polyester and a cover of sheeting type fabric.

Duvet   A comforter-type bed covering with a filling of goose down, the ultimate in warmth, lightness, and luxury.

Muslin   Plain weave fabric, originally all cotton, now often a blend of cotton and polyester, medium in weight.

Pillow sham   A decorative covering for a bed pillow, sometimes with a flounced, ruffled, or lace edge.

Percale   Fine, plain weave fabric of cotton yarns or cotton and polyester blend.

Bath Linens

Cam border   A plain, flat, patternless, side-to-side woven border at the hem ends of a towel, sometimes appearing as a design element running across the body of the towel.

Dobby border   A flat horizontal border, woven in a pattern of small geometric designs at or near the ends of a solid-colored towel.

Jacquard   A design woven into the fabric to create a three-dimensional effect, named for the French inventor of the jacquard loom and process.

Pile   The looped or sheared surface of a fabric, a distinguishing feature of terry cloth towels.

Sheared   The surface of a towel after its loops have been cut on one side leaving the other side looped, also called velour.

Terry cloth   The cotton, or cotton/polyester blend fabric of which most towels are made.

Velour   A sheared fabric with a napped finish from the French word meaning velvet.

Minimum requirements: For the bath - 3 body sheets, 3 bath towels, 6 washcloths, 3 hand towels for each person; plus 2 bath mats, 2 shower curtains and liners, and 6 guest hand towels. For the bedroom - 3 fitted and 3 flat sheets, 3 pillowcases (6 for queen), 2 pillows (4 for queen), 2 mattress pads, 2 mattress covers, 1 winter and 1 summer blanket, and 1 bedspread, or comforter and bedskirt, for each bed.

Table Linens

Applique   Precut decoration made separately, then sewn or embroidered onto a base cloth.

Batiste   A sheer, fine, combed cotton cloth, also made of rayon, polyester, and cotton blends.

Breakfast set   A placemat with one or two napkins, often used on breakfast trays.

Bridge set   A 39" x 39" tablecloth with four small napkins.

Cross stitch   A form of embroidery using two slanting stitches, one over the other to form an "x".

Cut work   Openwork embroidery in which the pattern is cut out and sewn on the ground cloth.

Doilies   Round and oval dressings for the table that can double as placemats in a 12" x 18" size or are simply used as decorative accents.

Damask   Made of linen, cotton, or rayon, and marked by a lustrous motif on a duller finish.

Drop   The distance between the top of the table and the hem of the tablecloth. The desired drop is between 6" and 12" on each side. In formal linens, a 12" to 14" drop is preferable.

Hemstitch   Ornamental stitching giving the effect of a row of stitching, used mostly on all-linen tablecloths.

Luncheon set   A 52" square, or 52" x 70" cloth with four to six 17" napkins.

Scarves   Decorative dressings for the table that are usually about 15" wide and in lengths that range from 30" to 60".

Tea set   A combination of a 44" x 44" tablecloth with four 14" matching napkins.

Trapunto   A type of quilting giving a high-relief effect.

Minimum requirements: 1 tablecloth of fine linen with 8 to 12 napkins; 2 everyday tablecloths with matching or contrasting napkins; 8 to 12 placemats with napkins.

Flatware

Flatware   Knives, forks, spoons, and serving pieces.

Hollowware   Serving pieces such as platters, bowls, and pitchers.

Pewter   Flatware and hollowware of a soft, silver gray metal made of a variety of tin alloys, with a polished or satin finish.

Pewterplate   Hollowware of a base metal electroplated with pewter.

Place Settings
   3-piece Starter   Teaspoon, Knife, and Fork

   4-piece Basic   Teaspoon, Knife, Fork, and Salad Fork

   5-piece Regular   Teaspoon, Knife, Fork, Salad Fork, and Place or Soup Spoon

   6-piece Formal   Teaspoon, Knife, Fork, Salad Fork, Place or Soup Spoon, Butter Spreader

Silverplate   Flatware and hollowware of a nonprecious metal, with a satin, mirror, or pewter finish.

Stainless steel   Flatware and hollowware of a nonprecious metal with a satin, mirror, or pewter finish.

The Wedding Gifts—A Colorful Lot

Sterling   Flatware and hollowware of solid silver, by law containing 92.5 parts pure silver to 7.5 parts alloy, frequently copper.

Sterling II   Flatware with hollow, sterling silver handles and stainless steel tines, bowls, and blades.

Vermeil   Flatware and hollowware of sterling silver electroplated with gold.

Minimum requirements: 8 knives, forks, salad forks, butter spreaders, cream soup spoons, dessert spoons; 16 teaspoons; 4 tablespoons; 1 cold meat fork, two-piece steak set, sugar spoon, gravy ladle, butter and cake knife.

Glassware

Colored glass   Glass made by mixing various kinds of minerals with the basic glass mixture.

Crystal   The colorless, sparkling quality of good glass.

Cut crystal   Crystal that has been expertly and intricately cut, then polished for light refraction and sparkle.

Lead crystal   Crystal with superior brilliance and weight, containing more lead than ordinary glass.

Milk glass   Opaque white glass, smoothly polished.

Opaline   Semi-opaque glass, more formal than milk glass.

Pressed glass   Glass formed in patterned molds to produce three dimensional, raised designs.

Suite   A crystal suite consists of a water goblet, wine glass, and champagne glass (flute or dessert/champagne). Iced beverage may be substituted for the water goblet.

Minimum requirements: 8 goblets, 8 wine glasses (preferably the red wine bowled style), 8 sherbert glasses, 8 champagne glasses (either flutes or dessert), and 8 cordial glasses.

Tableware

Bone china   Fine china containing bone ash to give it a characteristic whiteness.

Ceramic   Any molded and fired clayware.

Earthenware   Thick, opaque and porous ware made from clays that cannot withstand the high heat needed to produce the translucency of fine china, not vitrified.

Fine china   Term applying to china that is translucent and vitrified.

Glaze   A glasslike coating that is fired onto the ware to produce a glossy surface.

Hollowware   Another name for serving pieces.

Ironstone   A heavy earthenware.

Overglaze   Decorations applied on top of the glaze.

Porcelain   Fine dinnerware and decorative accessories, differing from china in the way it is manufactured.

Pottery   Informal decorative clay accessories or dinnerware, more rustic in appearance and more likely to chip.

Stoneware   Hard, nonporous ware.

Open stock   Refers to the fact that individual pieces of a pattern may be purchased at any time, as long as the manufacturer is still producing it.

Place setting   Assorted items in one pattern available for each person at the table. A 3-piece buffet setting consists of a dinner plate, teacup, and saucer. A 5-piece complete setting consists of a dinner, salad/dessert plate, bread and butter plate, teacup, and saucer.

Opaque   Nontranslucent, as earthenware or pottery.

Serving Set   A 5-piece serving set consists of a 16″ oval platter, a large open vegetable bowl, a cream pitcher, and a covered sugar bowl.

Translucent   Ware through which light can pass. Your hand can be seen clearly behind such a piece when it is held to the light.

Vitrified   Fine, nonporous china fired at extremely high temperatures, making it stronger, thinner and more translucent.

Minimum requirements: 8 ten-inch dinner plates; 8 six-inch bread and butter plates; 12 eight-inch salad or dessert plates; 8 cups and saucers and soup plates; 1 teapot, 1 cream and sugar, and 2 vegetable dishes.

*Bridal Lace, a
Laura Ashway
Design*

211

For Every Style
If you simply can't make up your mind which china to choose, you can't go wrong with these patterns. Borders of platinum and gold enhance plain white or ivory in these two patterns and can be used in any formal dining room.

The Wedding Gifts—A Colorful Lot

***Dramatic/
Neoclassic***
*Graced with
Greek motifs, the
Colonnade
pattern can be
used with any of
the formal
furniture styles
that influenced the
Federal period,
such as Sheraton,
Hepplewhite,
Directoire and
Empire.*

Photo: Courtesy Wedgwood

***Dramatic/
Art Deco***
*So influential in
the 20th century,
the decorative
style of Art Deco
has inspired
timeless and
sophisticated
patterns, such as
Amherst that will
enhance a
dramatic dining
room.*

Photo: Courtesy Wedgwood

Colors for Brides

213

Classic/English Traditional

Most celebrated of all English floral designs, rose patterns set in the traditional round shape can be used with any of the formal traditional English furniture styles, as long as they are in your colors.

Photo: Courtesy Lenox

Romantic/ Victorian

Inspired by Victorian design and interpreted in rich colors, the Coburg pattern will complement any dining room with the more formal Victorian furniture styles in dark woods.

Photo: Courtesy Hutchenreuther

The Wedding Gifts—A Colorful Lot

Romantic/ Early American The center decoration, floral rim, and scalloped shape of the River James pattern make it the perfect choice for a semiformal dining room with Queen Anne chairs.

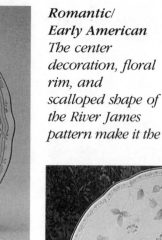

Romantic/Country French Overall floral patterns in the romantic, scalloped shape of Harris Grove complement a semiformal dining room with Country French furniture.

Romantic/Country Sculptured shapes with small floral patterns, such as Melody, can be used in less formal, but romantic, dining rooms or breakfast rooms with country furniture styles.

Colors for Brides

Casual
Informal china like Boulder Ridge is just right for Country

Contemporary or Southwestern style dining rooms or breakfast rooms.

A crystal suite consists of a water goblet, wine glass and champagne glass. This photo shows both kinds of champagne glass—dessert and flute. The dessert glass can be used

for both desserts, other than pastries, of course, and champagne. Look for brilliance, sheen, and clarity. Fine crystal has a bell-like ring when you tap the rim.

Photo: Courtesy Gorham

The Wedding Gifts—A Colorful Lot

Colonial American
Graceful, but understated, patterns such as Old Maryland Plain are at home in the city or in the suburbs, in dining rooms with Queen Anne or Colonial furniture.

English Chippendale
Curved, carved, fluted, and scrolled like the decorations on 18th century English furniture styles, Chippendale patterns can be used with formal traditional English furniture.

Colors for Brides

French Provincial *Delicately engraved patterns such as this French Provincial one can be used in formal dining rooms with 18th century French and Italian furniture styles.*

American Victorian *With its graceful lines, rococo scroll work, and rose motifs, this American Victorian pattern will complement the more formal Victorian furniture styles.*

The Wedding Gifts—A Colorful Lot

Baroque
Inspired by the Renaissance, Baroque patterns like El Grandee will complement the more ornate European furniture styles, whether Italian, French, or Spanish.

Contemporary
Inspired by 19th century motifs, and updated for today, contemporary patterns such as Woodwind will fit into almost any room.

Colors for Brides

A formal tablesetting with a dramatic flair using all your tableware, flatware, and crystal. The china is Wedgwood's Ulander Ruby. Designed by Angelo Bonita, Washington Harbour Flowers. Contributing designer and photographer: Paul Douzmati, AIFD, Nielsen's Florist, Darien, CT.

The Wedding Gifts—A Colorful Lot

Chapter 12
A New Address

Moving In

After all the festivities are over and you've returned from your honeymoon, you and your new husband will be eager to build your "nest." Whether it is a tiny first apartment or townhouse, or a huge estate, you want it to be a comfortable place to begin your new life together.

If one of you is moving in with the other, you'll have some furnishings to start with. And, of course, there are all your wedding gifts to put on shelves, beds, and tables. Now, how do you blend these elements together and start a decorating scheme that reflects both of your personalities and color palettes?

As I said in my previous book, *Your Colors at Home* (Acropolis Books, 1985), decorating has always caused a faint tremble in the bottom of even the most stalwart heart. Decisions about style and color that we make for ourselves in a split-second become monumental when they're going to be spread all over a room or shared with someone as special as your new husband.

It takes a combination of courage and expertise to design and furnish a room, so think about what you are about to do—furnish an entirely new apartment or house so that both you and your husband feel happy. You'll be spending quite a bit of money; decorating mistakes can't be hidden in a closet. And, everyone who comes into your new home will be able to see and judge the colors and style you've decided upon. You are probably more of an expert at choosing your own clothes than your own furnishings.

But don't worry, this chapter will help you look at your palette, consider your style, and choose the types of furnishings, wall and floor coverings that are going to make your new home a beautiful place for the two of you.

As Always—Start with Color

You know your color season and your husband's. If you are lucky, they are both the same and there will be no question of which colors to choose. If you are both cool seasons or warm seasons, again you are lucky. Go with the warm or the cool palettes. They'll blend beautifully. But if one of you is a cool season and the other is warm, go with yours, using some of his as accents or in the room he uses most. Study both palettes and look for colors you may have in common, and use these whenever possible.

Or, if you are a true peacemaker, there are three colors you can choose as a decorating base that can be flattering to everyone. They are *aqua, periwinkle* and *coral pink.*

Almost all of us look good in schemes based on these three colors when they are liberally laced with white. Whose white? Probably the all-around best compromise between seasons is the off-white of Summer.

There are three ways to use these "season-spanner" colors. You and your husband can choose which of the three you like best and use it with off-white. Or try a related scheme of aqua and periwinkle with off-white, or a contrasting scheme of coral pink and either aqua or periwinkle and off-white. Or find a print that has all three colors on an off-white background.

But let's hope you have the flexibility to use many of the colors in your palette and aren't restricted to the peacemaker palette. Look at each palette again.

Much of the advice in this chapter is taken from *Your Colors at Home.* I've condensed it and adapted it to your "beginning a new life together" situation, but I do suggest you read *Your Colors at Home* for a complete decorating guide. There is a coupon at the back of the book so you can order right from the publisher, at a special bridal discount.

Seasonal Decorating Styles

Just as we did for your wedding, let's consider your personal style now. It is this plus your palette that will determine your decorating plan.

You may already have noticed, that frequently the Winter is the ultraformal, dramatic type. Somehow their high contrasts lead to dramatic effects the other seasons can't share. Winters opt for sharp contrasts, such as black-and-white floors; and grand gestures, such as sweeping staircases, mahogany four poster beds, or an ultra contemporary ambience sparked with glass and chrome. Winter's rooms should be exciting, stimulating places: mirrors, lacquered wood, silver and crystal will make them shine. Sharp-edged geometrics and dynamic solids, and Oriental rugs, velvet and brocade, the Winter style is ultraformal. Winters look wonderful in rooms filled with color, or conversely, in all white rooms accented here and there with a few dynamite colors. Winter's best woods are dark with fine graining and a highly polished finish. Painted woods should be white or the true colors of the Winter palette. Their best metal is silver, or silver-toned.

Softer Summers tend toward the classic, focusing on periods that are formal, but less dramatic. Furniture with elegant, soft lines and gracefully curving legs can be part of your well-bred furnishings. Easy elegance is the key. Summers are a softer version of Winter. The same cool, blue tones underlie Summer's palette, and contrast is again a key word in planning color schemes. Only with Summers, the contrast is lighter, less resounding, more refined. Summers are mediators and their best colors are muted, gentled versions of Winter's attention-demanding palette. Summer's rooms are comfortable and relaxing, likely to be filled with period pieces—possibly French—and decidedly feminine. Their best woods have ashen overtones and low-gloss finishes. Painted woods should be off-white, a neutral, or one of your light colors. Summer's best metal is silver or rose-gold.

Springs are the semiformals, the romantics who can skip from whimsy to sophistication in one hop. Eighteenth and nineteenth century English and American styles or contemporary furnishings light in scale, Springs need furniture that is as fun-loving, fresh, and vivacious as they are. Spring's color message is fresh, bright, clear and everywhere laced with the cheery yellow of warm sunshine. Spring's crisp colors are inherently alive and sunny. Look for a touch of whimsy in their interiors, too, such as an amusing Victorian piece, or a very romantic canopy bed, with ruffles on her boudoir chaise, and bright flowers everywhere. Springs are more interested in fun than formality. They may be sophisticated enough to pair painted chairs with a scrubbed pine dining table, but it will be done with uninhibited ease. The best wood colors for Springs are light golden blonde to medium golden brown, with a semi-gloss finish. Painted woods should be ivory, or in Spring's bright colors. Their best metal is polished brass.

Then we have those informal, natural Autumns. Look for comfort, furnishings that are as down-to-earth, as easy-living as you are. Country pieces or comfortably-scaled contemporary, these are the mellow styles for the nature-loving Autumn, whose colors too reflect this vibrant season with its soft golden days, full of brilliant leaves turning to brown, pumpkins, mums, and apple cider. Autumns bring the outdoors indoors with rooms you feel instantly at home in: friendly, welcoming, and very easy to relax in. Autumn's best woods are medium-to-dark brown with a low-gloss or antiqued finish. Painted woods should be oyster, neutrals, or medium-to-dark colors. Their best metal is antiqued brass.

Ultraformal Winter, Formal Summer, Semiformal Spring, or Informal Autumn, here are your decorating styles at a glance...

Decorating Styles at a Glance

	Dramatic	**Classic**	**Romantic**	**Natural**
Winter	Oriental Art Deco Modern Contemporary Eclectic Mix	Formal English Formal French	Formal Victorian French Provincial	Early English Early American Southwestern Contemporary Casual
Summer	Contemporary Eclectic Mix	Formal English Formal French	Formal Victorian French Provincial	Early American Contemporary Casual
Autumn	Contemporary Eclectic Mix	Formal English Formal French	Farmhouse Victorian French Country	Early English Early American Southwestern Contemporary Casual
Spring	Contemporary Eclectic Mix	Formal English Formal French	French Provincial Cottage Victorian American Country	Early American Contemporary Casual

Put Your Palette into a Plan

Now we are ready to push up our sleeves and get down to the real planning, with your palette and personality ready to color it in.

Buy yourself some graph paper where the scale is one-quarter inch to one foot of floor space. If you really want to be professional about all this, you can purchase furniture templates in the same scale at an art supply store. (Or order a set of templates with the coupon at the back of this book.) Measure your rooms with a metal rule and mark off their dimensions on the graph paper. Be sure to note all permanent features: doors, windows, fireplace, built-ins, and electrical outlets.

Now put in place the pieces of furniture you have. Unless you are planning to change the fabrics, color in the colors. Now where are the holes? Do you have a "dowry" from your husband? How does his black wool Scandinavian modern sofa go with your pink silk Queen Anne chair? What about Grandmother Todd's firescreen? Or your mother and father's recreation room sofa? What if your graph paper is empty?

It won't be for long. As you make your purchases, or look at them in furniture and decorating stores, "try" them in your rooms by using the appropriate template for furniture or placing a small piece of the fabric or wallcovering into your "room." Do you like the overall effect when you've put the paint chips, fabric, floorcovering, and wallcovering swatches together with your furniture pieces? You should be able to tell at a glance when you look at this little room—before you make the big purchase, not when it is sitting unhappily in the real room.

Furniture

Fashions in home furnishings come and go, just as they do in clothing. But no matter how much time goes by, the good design of each period—traditional or contemporary—will still be good, and will adapt to new looks with a little refurbishing.

When you shop for furniture, you'll note that it is marketed in "suites," "groups," and "collections." A *suite* consists of basic pieces designed to be used together in one room. All the pieces look alike and are priced as a unit. For instance, a dining room suite consists of a table, chairs, and buffet; a bedroom suite includes a bed, dresser, and a chest.

A *group,* on the other hand, consists of a "family" of furniture with the same design style for every room, including the basic suite plus many additional pieces. The advantage of purchasing a suite or a starter group is that you can add extra pieces from it as your budget and space expands. The disadvantage is that you might wind up with a monotonous room if you are not very clever with accessories.

A *collection* is usually a little more expensive, but each piece in the design group has a look of individuality. Designs have a feeling of compatibility, but are not exactly the same. Your final room will look as if it were made up of individual pieces collected over a period of time, instead of all purchased as a unit.

In purchasing furniture, *style* refers to the use of certain design characteristics. *Period* designates a time in history when these design characteristics were popular. Sometimes furniture styles are divided into *traditional* and *contemporary. Traditional* usually includes those styles with design characteristics typical of master craftsmen of past generations, i.e., Queen Anne, Sheraton, Chippendale, and Hepplewhite. Much traditional furniture was first designed for kings and queens. That is why traditional furniture is considered more formal. Simplified versions of these court styles are referred to as provincial or country styles, such as Early American or French Provincial. They are much less formal. Contemporary refers to more *modern* design characteristics, adapted to modern methods of production and lifestyle. Comtemporary can be inspired by traditional styles, while modern has no trace of the past.

Today there are no strict rules on how furniture is combined. Mixing the past with the present requires a little expertise. You can mix them if you use your palette—of woods, fabrics, colors, textures, and styles. A few terms you should understand ...

- antique - at least 100 years old

- reproduction - a line-for-line copy of an antique

- adaptation - a copy of some of the elements of a particular period, adapted to fit present-day needs

Just remember that the reproductions of today are the antiques of tomorrow.

I recommend purchasing each piece of new furniture as if it were a separate part of your grand plan. Look for quality and design. Don't feel you have to buy everything at once. And, don't feel that you need to choose everything in one period. Think instead of your palette and your lifestyle and pick pieces that fit both. Are you an ultraformal Winter? Don't purchase a contemporary teak dining table even if it is on sale. It simply won't fit your decorating scheme. Are you a semiformal, romantic Spring? Don't buy that big oak armoire, it will dwarf your other more delicate furnishings. Are you a formal Summer? Don't buy that sleek, sectioned leather sofa. It just won't wear well for you in the years ahead. Are you an informal, nature-loving Autumn? Don't buy that brocade wing chair. You won't sit in it. Remember your style, remember your colors, remember your ultimate plan.

Your first essential purchase must be a bed or beds. Whatever size you decide upon, buy the best quality mattress and box springs. Purchase the headboard later on, if necessary. Consider a wicker headboard, or a faux canopy made from sheets hung from a ceiling-mounted rod, or a padded headboard slipcovered to match your comforter. After all, your bed is the focal point of this most personal and intimate room in your new life. And, since more of your skin will be showing here than almost any other room, be sure that the colors are in your palette! The only other essential piece of furniture for your bedroom is a storage piece: a chest, armoire, or highboy. This is an expensive purchase. Think of your plan before you purchase. Now draw these pieces onto your graph paper.

Next, you'll need to eat together. So you need a table and chairs. Consider the space you have to work with when selecting your table, be it round, square, or rectangular. A painted parson's table in one of your season's colors is always a good choice. Even if you replace it later on with a more formal table, it can be used in another room or even as a desk. It is one of those classics you can afford right away. But, if you don't have room for a rectangular table, look for a drop-leaf in one of your woods. Sometimes you can find an antique or "used" one at a very reasonable price. It takes little space, especially when its sides are dropped; and later on it can be used in another room as an end table or between two chairs or in your bedroom for intimate meals together. You may want to invest in four good side chairs. Later on, when you have more space, you can get a better table and add uphostered host and hostess chairs.

What about the living room? Where will your guests sit? Rather than buy a roomful of budget furniture, carefully select one good piece at a time. Start with a sofa in one of the furniture styles for your season, or a straight arm Tuxedo or round arm Lawson which will go with almost any style of furniture.

If you have a small space, start with a love seat. Buy the matching bigger sofa later. Fill the rest of the room with plants and pillows until you can buy the chairs, or bring in the dining room chairs when guests arrive.

All you really need in the beginning is a bed, a chest, a table and chairs, and a sofa. Just remember these general guidelines as you add to your collection . . .

- One style of furniture should dominate, but a few well-chosen pieces of another style will add interest.

- Pieces of about the same characteristics and scale can be compatible, even if they are in another period.

- Woods should be mixed with care. Formal mahogany, for instance, does not mix with scrubbed pine. They're in different seasons, too.

Fabric

A quick way to make the furniture you are bringing to the marriage blend with his furniture is to recover it in your chosen seasonal palette.

After color, patterns most affect the way things go together, so these general guidelines will be helpful. Patterns used within the same room should have a common denominator, which means that one or more of the elements, such as color, texture, or pattern, running throughout, will give a feeling of harmony and unity to the room. That is certainly a goal you have in your first house.

The principal pattern need not be repeated in the room as long as one or more of the colors are carried over into another area. A floral print of rose and blue gray on the sofa can be enhanced by rose and blue-gray pillows, for instance. Or repeat the same pattern on several pieces of furniture and at the windows, with accessories in the accent colors.

A room should have no more than one large pattern of the same type of design, such as floral. Once the dominant pattern is established, supplement it with a small pattern—a stripe, a check, a plaid, or plain fabrics.

When you are combining patterned fabrics, scale should be considered. For example, if a large floral print is combined with a plaid or a stripe or both, they must also be large in scale. If a small floral pattern is used, then the other fabrics should not overpower the basic pattern. Two patterns that are similar can work well together, but they must be alike in color but not alike in scale—a large plaid and a small shadow check, or a large floral and a smaller coordinating floral, for example.

Decorating on a Small Budget?

Try using sheets. The cost will be just a fraction of decorating a comparable room with standard fabric. You can now find sheets in almost any color, from pretty pastels to vivid jewels tones . . .and in all types of patterns, from florals to plaids, to stripes, checks, and dots—and all pattern sizes, from mini-prints to mid-scale and large-scale choices.

Most sheets come with matching comforters and bedskirts. If the pattern you choose does not, you can make a duvet cover and bedskirt. You can slipcover your headboard, make matching curtains or shades, a dressing-table skirt, a dressing screen, and even cover picture frames and desk accessories with leftover fabric.

In a dining room, use a large-scale patterned sheet to cover your walls above a chair rail. Use a smaller coordinating sheet for curtains or shades, and for tie-on chair cushions. You can even make table cloths, place mats, and napkins.

In the living room, use solid-color and patterned sheets to make slipcovers, pillows, and curtains or shades. Use a patterned sheet to make a floor cloth. And, use your patterned sheet or fabric to set your color scheme. Take the background color of the fabric and use it on the walls and for the sofa, use the patterned sheet at windows and for chairs, use the most eye-catching color as an accent.

Now you have the basics, but if you need more help, order *Your Colors at Home* at your bookstore or send in the coupon at the back of this book. This book will give you much more information on room arrangements and accessories, as well as the many different types of furniture, fabrics, wallcoverings, and floorcoverings suitable for each season.

Queen Anne

Until the mid-18th century, it was customary to name furniture styles after the reigning king or queen. Queen Anne was the last English monarch associated by name with a furniture style and the Queen Anne style was the first formal style in England.

Photo: Courtesy Kittinger

A typical Queen Anne highboy displays this style's most identifiable feature, the cabriole leg.

The still popular high wing-back chair was originally designed to protect one's head from the draft.

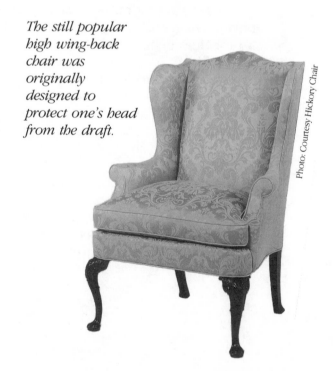

Photo: Courtesy Hickory Chair

Chippendale

When Thomas Chippendale introduced his innovative designs, he used his own name. But there were two King Georges during the 18th century and, in order to keep them happy, the term Georgian was also used to describe Chippendale furniture.

Photo: Courtesy Hickory Chair

Chippendale's version of the highboy.

Photo: Courtesy Smith & Watson

Chippendale dining room chair.

Photo: Courtesy Kittinger

The camelback is the most popular of all the Chippendale upholstered pieces and was named for the high arch resembling a camel's back.

Hepplewhite

George Hepplewhite was an English cabinetmaker who became famous during the Georgian period and his designs are still being copied today.

The curved back and straight, tapered arms and legs are the identifiable features of the Hepplewhite love seat.

Photo: Courtesy Kittinger

Photo: Courtesy Kittinger

The Hepplewhite sideboard reached its height in popularity during the Federal period and is still a favorite in today's formal dining rooms.

A New Address

Sheraton

Thomas Sheraton, a cabinetmaker during the Georgian period, is considered second only to Chippendale.

Photo: Courtesy Hickory Chair

Characterized by its rectilinear frame and reeded legs, the Sheraton loveseat reflects the changing tastes in styles during the late 18th century.

The double pedestal table is probably the most popular of all the Sheraton furniture styles being made today and mixes well with Chippendale chairs.

Photo: Courtesy Smith & Watson

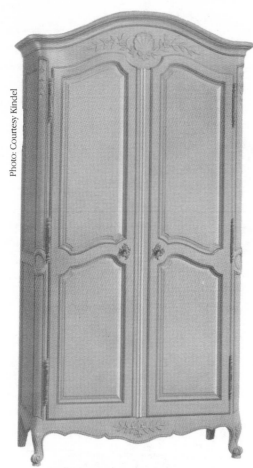

Louis XV

The most popular 18th century French styles are those of the romantic Louis XV era, characterized by curved lines and fine woods with delicate carving.

Once used for storing armour or tools, the versatile armoire can be used for storing clothes, as an entertainment center, or even as a bar.

Widely used today as an occasional, or pull-up chair the Louis XV open armchair can be used in any room of the house.

Louis XVI

The Louis XVI era brought back Italian-like classic lines and is sometimes referred to as Italian Provincial.

Characterized by an oval padded back and arms and straight fluted legs, the Louis XVI open armchair is popular in living rooms. Armless versions of this style mix beautifully with glass dining room tables.

Photo: Courtesy Ethan Allan

Photo: Courtesy Henredon

Another popular version of this style features a square padded back with loose cushions.

235

French Country

French Country furniture is copied from styles originally made by the peasants in 18th century France. Most of the pieces follow the lines of the Louis XV style but are simpler and woods are distressed.

Photo: Courtesy Guy Chaddock

A simple four drawer French Country chest can serve many purposes.

Photo: Courtesy Guy Chaddock

The ladder back chair remains the most popular French Country chair and is identifiable by its salamander back, simple curved leg and rush seat.

A New Address

Early English

There are several styles that make up Early English furniture, including Jacobean, Tudor and the popular William and Mary style which was introduced just prior to Queen Anne.

Photo: Courtesy Guy Chaddock

The four drawer chest has bracket feet, which were first used in the William and Mary period.

Photo: Courtesy Smith & Watson

A typical ladder back side chair with turned legs, stretcher, and rush seat can be used in any room with English Country furniture.

Early American

Many of the Early English pieces were brought to the American Colonies and were the origin of the Early American style.

Courtesy Nichols & Stone

Adapted from the earlier English style, one of the most popular versions of the ladder back chair has four slats and spool-turned legs, rounds and pillars.

Photo: Courtesy Wright Table Co.

The bow back Windsor chair was first made in

Windsor, England and brought to New England by the Pilgrims. Variations of the chair have been made in this country ever since.

Photo: Courtesy Nichols & Stone

Open cupboards were especially popular with the German settlers in Pennsylvania

and even today can be used in any informal dining or family room.

Victorian

The Victorian period introduced the first eclectic look in decorating. The mood varied from formal and pretentious to cottage to farmhouse.

Photo: Courtesy Hickory Chair

Originally used in Victorian farmhouses as a washstand, a chest like this can be used in a bedroom or dining room.

Wicker became popular in the mid-19th century as the Victorians began to build summer cottages at the shore.

Photo: Courtesy O'Asian Designs, Inc.

Photo: Courtesy Hickory Chair

The rolled back rail and arm, and soft pleated dressmaker skirt are the identifying features of the formal Victorian chair.

Modern

The term modern is usually applied to furniture styles of the 1920's that originated at the Bauhaus School of Art and Architecture.

Made of leather with x-shaped steel supports, the Barcelona chair was designed by the architect Mies van der Rohe.

Photo: Courtesy Knoll

Photo: Courtesy Knoll

Designed by Marcel Breuer and named for his daughter, the Cesca chair is made of tubular steel with cane seat and back.

Charles Eames designed the contour lounge chair and ottoman made with moulded plywood and leather.

Photo: Courtesy Herman Miller

A Glossary of Furniture Styles

Formal Traditional

Queen Anne   A furniture style named after Queen Anne, who ruled England for just twelve years from 1702 to 1714, but who is immortalized in design history by the graceful furniture she favored. Furniture lines are curved and arms and legs are slender. Cabriole legs and chairs with fiddle backs are typical. Shell carvings are common. Woods are walnut and mahogany.

Colonial/American Georgian   The period from 1700–1781. Also called American Georgian, it is the era personified by Colonial Williamsburg. Furniture of Chippendale, Hepplewhite and Sheraton is typical. Lines are both straight and curved. Chairbacks are ladder, pierced splat, shield, oval, or square. Woods are walnut, mahogany, and stainwood.

Federal   Furniture style that flourished in America after the Revolution (about 1781–1830) influenced by England (Hepplewhite and Sheraton) and France (Directoire and Empire). Duncan Phyfe, a New York cabinetmaker, interpreted the designs but developed a style of his own. Paw and claw feet and carved arms and legs are typical. Mahogany is common.

Louis XV   Furniture style named after Louis XV—or Louis Quinze (kanz)—King of France from 1715–1774, whose reign is synonymous with rococo. Furniture with curved legs, backs and arms joined in continuous curves, and scroll carving is typical. Woods are usually walnut or fruitwood.

Louis XVI (also known as Italian Provincial)   Furniture style named after Louis XVI—or Louis Seize (sez)—King of France from 1774–1793, who during his reign brought back straight lines and classic motifs. Legs are often fluted or carved. Chairs with wood frames, padded oval backs and padded arms are typical. Woods are walnut, mahogany, and satinwood.

Less Formal Traditional

Early English   The furniture of 17th century England covers a wide range of moods in varying degrees of formality. Furniture is robust and legs are usually turned with shaped stretchers often set between the feet. Gateleg tables, spindle-back chairs and Welsh cupboards are typical. Walnut is the most common wood.

Early American   The furniture of the first settlers in the New World (1608–1720) is a simplified version of 17th century English styles. Furniture is sturdy; ladder-back chairs, open hutches, and cobbler's benches are typical. Most common woods are maple, oak, and pine.

French Country   Simplified version of the 18th century French styles that were being made in the more sophisticated cities. Furniture lines are a combination of straight and curved. Chairs with salamander backs, armoires with molded panels, commodes with "chicken-wire" grills are typical. Distressed woods are common.

Other Styles

Victorian   Not a style of furniture but an era that spanned the 64-year reign of Queen Victoria of England and the first two decades of the 20th century. During that time, styles from Gothic to Greek were revived. Furniture lines are mostly curved. Decorations are ornate. Marble-topped tables, buttoned upholstery is common. Woods range all the way from dark mahogany to golden oak to white wicker.

Southwest   Composed of a blend of Spanish and Indian cultures, furniture of the Southwest is casual and unpretentious. Trestle tables, rush-bottom chairs, and the "trastero" or great cupboard are typical pieces. Furniture is handcarved and usually scrubbed, stained, or painted.

Modern   Furniture designs that completely depart from designs of the past and are characterized by the form-follows-function design that began in the Bauhaus such as Barcelona and Breuer chairs. Danish modern and Japanese styles are also typical.

Contemporary   Furniture designed and made today of today's materials. Lines are curved or straight. Forms are borrowed from various periods but made functional for today's living. Wall units and other dual-purpose furniture are typical.

American Country   A nostalgic attitude that began in the 1960s and swept the country, paralleling the overall back-to-basics movement. Open cupboards, ladder-back chairs, and blanket chests are typical. Scrubbed pine or painted finishes in buttermilk colors and stencil designs are common.

Chapter 13
Your Bridal Gift Register

Use this chapter to record your wedding gifts as they arrive. Be sure to record when you wrote the thank-you note. Review this record before your wedding so that you'll be able to thank people personally as they go through the receiving line, if you have one, at your reception.

You'll enjoy looking back over your gift list in years to come. I still remember many of the people who gave me gifts and think of them when I use their gift twenty years later.

Gift Description	Donor	Where Bought	Date Arrived	Note Written

Gift Description	Donor	Where Bought	Date Arrived	Note Written

Gift Description	Donor	Where Bought	Date Arrived	Note Written

Gift Description	Donor	Where Bought	Date Arrived	Note Written

Index

Many thanks,

for information, photographs, and encouragement,

to . . .

Bridalwear
Bridal Originals
Christos
House of Bianchi
LoVece, Ltd.
McCall Pattern Company
Ora Feder
Priscilla of Boston
Simplicity Pattern Co.
Vogue/Butterick

Cakes
Sylvia Weinstock Cakes, Ltd.
Ridgewell's Caterer

Formal Wear
After Six Formals
Raffinati

Flowers
Diana Love
Paul Duzmati
Frank Delio

Home Furnishings
Guy Chaddock
Ethan Allen
Henredon
Hickory Chair
Hub Furniture Centers
Kindel
Kittinger
Knoll
Nichols & Stone
O'Asian
Smith & Watson
Suter's
Wright Table Co.

Linens & Domestics
J. P. Stevens Co.

Tableware
Gorham
Hutchenreuther
Johnson Bros.
Kirk Stieff
Lenox
Lunt
Noritake
Reed & Barton
Towle
Wedgwood

THE ASSOCIATION OF BRIDAL CONSULTANTS

...an international trade organization serving the professionals in the bridal/ wedding business.

*F*ounded in 1981, ABC replaced the American Association of Professional Bridal Consultants, which had served the needs of wedding professionals from 1955.

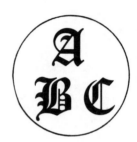

The Association offers a variety of services to its members, including:

- a newsletter
- seminars and workshops
- professional development programs
- national and local publicity and media referrals
- discounts on wedding-related materials
- national and local advertising
- referrals of brides
- an information service

For more information about the Association or for a list of members in your area, contact:

ASSOCIATION OF BRIDAL CONSULTANTS
Dept. C
200 Chestnutland Road
New Milford CT 06776-2521

If you are planning a wedding, please include your phone number, wedding date and a self-addressed, stamped, legal size envelope.

Members agree to uphold a Code of Ethics and Standards of Membership.

Help with Your Wedding Plans!

Many products are described in *Colors for Brides* which can help you with your wedding plans and with decorating your first home.

Check off your needs and return this coupon right away. We'll see that you receive your products in plenty of time to make your wedding a great success.

Yes, please send me . . .

QTY	ITEM	PRICE	TOTAL
	Purse-sized Fan Deck of 200 Seasonal Colors Perfect for shopping for every item you need for your wedding, your trousseau, and your first home. Check your season. ☐ Winter ☐ Summer ☐ Spring ☐ Autumn	$16. each	
	Wedding-in-a-Box Planner Planner, organizer and file in one box. A unique color-coded system, containing time tables, special service cards from flowers to food, individual guest cards, more.	$18. each	
	Wedding Day Makeup Kit Look your most beautiful on this day of days, using your season's makeup in this purse-size kit. Contains two lipsticks, two blushes, four eyeshadows, and applicators. Check your season. ☐ Winter ☐ Summer ☐ Spring ☐ Autumn	$16. each	
	Your Colors at Home The book that will help you decorate your first home in your own seasonal color palette and style. Written by Lauren Smith and Rose Gilbert, here is everything you need to know about furnishings, wall and floor coverings!	$13. each	
	Furniture Templates A set of 700 easy-to-use (and reuse) push-out furniture symbols, graph paper, and instructions help you plan how you want to arrange your first home. Avoid mistakes when you know how everything fits into your new space.	$16. each	
	Wedding Consultant Ready for professional help in planning any and every aspect of your wedding? Check here to receive a list of Lauren Smith consultants in your area.*	No charge	
	A More Colorful Career Think you're ready to become a consultant yourself? Check here to receive information about opportunities for qualified applicants in your geographical area.*	No charge	
	*Please enclose stamped self-addressed envelope.	**TOTAL**	

☐ My check is enclosed.   ☐ Charge to my ☐ VISA ☐ MC

Charge Card No. _____ Exp. date _____

NAME _____

ADDRESS _____

CITY _____ STATE _____ ZIP _____

Make check payable and mail to:
LAUREN SMITH, INC., c/o Acropolis Books Ltd., 2400 17th St., N.W., Washington, D.C. 20009